JAPANESE ARMS AND ARMOUR

Ian Bottomley

CONTENTS

Front cover: Detail of
a *haramaki* from the
Edo period. xxvia.213

Page 1: A *tsuba*
representing a goose
and clouds against
the moon. xxvis.373

Page 3: Map of Japan.
Mountain High Maps™ ©1995
Digital Wisdom, Inc.

Back cover: A *wakizashi*
and scabbard. xxvis.198

Kunashiri
(Kunashir)

Nemuro
Peninsula

HOKKAIDŌ
(EZO)

Sapporo

Oshima
Peninsula

Tsugaru Strait Peninsula

Shimokita
Peninsula

Akita

Sendai

H O N S H U

Sado

Noto
Peninsula

Tokyo
(Edo)

Bōsō
Peninsula

Izu Islands

Lake Biwa

Kyōto
(Miyako)

Kii
Peninsula

Ōsaka

Hachijō-jima

Shimonoseki

Inland Sea

SHIKOKU

KYŪSHŪ

Nagasaki

Tanegashima

INTRODUCTION

Almost from its inception, traditional Japan was a society ruled by a military elite. It is hardly surprising therefore that arms and armour played an important role in its culture. During the 17th century the country cut itself off from the world and what little knowledge there was of Japan in the West was largely forgotten. Following the country's opening in the 19th century, we have rediscovered the remarkable story of the development of Japan's weapons and armour, something this introductory book sets out for the general reader.

Ian Bottomley
Curator Emeritus, Royal Armouries

NOTES ON JAPANESE

The specialised terminology associated with Japanese arms and armour can be daunting, not least because a written character when used in an arms and armour context can have a different meaning or pronunciation from its everyday use. Where there is an English equivalent it will be used, but in many cases there will not be one and no alternative but to use Japanese. To assist the reader and prevent the possible confusion with some English words, Japanese terms will be printed in italics. All of the Japanese words used in the book are included in the glossary.

Pronouncing Japanese is not difficult. The vowels are similar to those in the Italian words 'cappuccino' and 'espresso', although the 'u' is hardly voiced. Vowels in Japanese can be of double length, but these have been omitted here. Consonants are pronounced very much as in English, but always with the hard 'g' as in 'go'. The reader should also be aware that many words in Japanese change their initial consonant in compounds when preceded by a word ending in a vowel – for example, *gusoku* (armour) and *hitsu* (box) becomes *gusoku bitsu* when read as 'an armour box'. In these cases the meaning is the same, the consonant change being simply to ease pronunciation. Finally, you should note that the Japanese place their family name before their personal name, a convention retained here.

LACQUER

Throughout this book reference is made to lacquer, a material totally unlike the paints, varnishes and so-called 'lacquers' used in the West. Real lacquer or *urushi* is obtained from the tree, *Toxicodendron vernicifluum*, by making cuts in the trunk and scraping off the viscous sap as it exudes. After processing, the sap forms an aqueous varnish that hardens irreversibly when exposed to warm moist conditions forming a hard, dark brown, flexible, waterproof coating that cannot be dissolved by solvents and is not affected by acids or alkalis.

The process of lacquering is complex involving multiple base coats made from raw lacquer mixed with fillers such as rice flour, clay and powdered stone and then multiple layers of pigmented finishing lacquer. The range of pigments that can be used is very limited. Black is obtained using either carbon or reacting raw *urushi* with iron compounds. Reds involve mixing lacquer with either iron oxide or vermilion. A gilded finish can be obtained by applying gold as either leaf or dust to wet lacquer. Often the final coats will be simply polished to a gloss but by texturing the base coats or adding materials such as sawdust, chopped straw or mother of pearl to the finishing coats, all manner of textures and decorative effects can be created.

▲ An armourer's workshop. The man in the right foreground is lacquering parts, whilst on the left they are being polished. From a reproduction of a 16th-century screen

THE CLASSICAL PERIOD (TO 1467)

The people we know as Japanese arrived on the Japanese archipelago from Central Asia in a series of invasions during the first millennium of our era, bringing with them the horses and the arms and armour of their homelands that they used to drive the aboriginal inhabitants northwards. It was natural that this fledgling nation should look to China for inspiration, adopting Buddhism and applying the Chinese system of writing to express their own language. By the end of the first millennium a unique, sophisticated culture had evolved centred around the emperor's court in the city we now know as Kyoto.

Elsewhere in the country, minor members of the nobility managed the various provinces, collecting taxes, maintaining order and, if the need arose, donning armour and fighting for one or another faction at court. It was this social group who were to become the military class or *buke*, individual members being known as *bushi* or more commonly *samurai* – a name derived from an ancient court title meaning 'one who serves'.

◀ *Opposite*: Detail of *akodanari* helmet.
XXVIA.1

◀ A *samurai* and his wife unpacking an armour from its storage box. I.303

Another powerful force were the Buddhist temples who maintained their own troops, nominally described as novices, to look after their often extensive territorial interests. Inevitably there were rivalries between the various armed groups, culminating in the late-12th century in open warfare between the two of the most powerful *samurai* clans, the Minamoto and the Taira. Victory for the Minamoto, in what was known as the Genpei wars from the Chinese reading of their names, resulted in their leader, Minamoto Yoritomo, being given the greater powers to collect taxes and appoint stewards and constables around the country. To avoid the soft life of the capital weakening the resolve of his forces, he set up his military court in distant Kamakura. In 1192, the then Emperor Go-Toba granted Yoritomo the ancient title of *Sei-i tai Shogun*, or 'Barbarian-suppressing commander', generally shortened to *shogun*. Successive *shoguns* took even more powers to themselves leaving Kyoto to become little more than a ceremonial centre occupied by an emperor who had almost no influence on matters of state and spent his time undertaking religious and other rituals.

HORSES

During these early wars the horse was an essential part of a *samurai's* equipment. Battles began with individuals shouting their pedigrees and previous exploits before charging at a selected opponent, shooting their arrows before wheeling their horses and returning to their own lines. It was only after these arrow duels had finished that the sides would join and fight with swords. Throughout these encounters the task of the *samurai's* retainers, who were on foot, was to assist their lord should he become unhorsed.

Genetics show that the various breeds of traditional Japanese horses are not indigenous but derive from a common ancestor related to the sturdy horses of the Asian steppes. Because most Japanese were Buddhist who ate little or no meat, strong leather from which to make their harnesses was in very short supply; consequently a large part of a Japanese harness is made from textiles. Suitable straps could be made from folded hemp cloth, generally covered in

▲ Mounted *samurai* and his attendants, from an 18th-century book on armour, *Gun yo ki* by Ise Sadatake. Private collection

a more decorative fabric. An alternative was to braid silk around a core of hemp threads to produce a heavy, round cord so that when several are sewn together side by side they produce a strap of adequate strength.

During this early period a harness would consist only of these straps, but in later times they were embellished by adding panels of knotted cords and long fringes of silk threads that hung around the horse rather like a European caparison. Most harnesses were dyed bright red, but blue and purple ones were also produced.

▶ A typical Edo period harness, from a display at the Royal Amouries Museum, Leeds. XXVIA.45, XXVIH.42, M.1935, AL.268-5

A typical harness would consist of an iron bit of broken snaffle type and a bridle of fabric straps that terminated in tasselled ends fastened to loops on the cheek-pieces of the bit. The reins were usually a folded length of white cotton cloth dyed with blue stripes, the ends being bunched together and fastened to arms on the bit. The saddle, or *kura*, was constructed around a wooden saddletree made from four pieces of red oak. The pommel and cantle at the front and back of the saddle were cut from trees that had been bent into a 'U'-shape as saplings so the grain of the wood followed the curve. Connecting these were two sidepieces joined by ties of hemp cord so that the saddle could flex with the movement of the horse. Most saddletrees were extravagantly lacquered and decorated with the owner's heraldry.

Under the legs of the saddle-tree were leather-faced fabric pads to protect the horse, whilst at the front and back were rings to which a breast strap and a crupper strap were fastened to prevent the saddle shifting out of place. Hanging on leather straps were heavy iron stirrups or *abumi*, shaped like a boot without sides and decorated with lacquer or inlay in gold or silver.

When shooting his bow a *samurai* would stand on the stirrups, lifting himself off the saddle to avoid the jolting of the horse beneath him. Later harnesses had two large leather panels hung below the saddle called *aori gawa* that, as the name implies, kept the rider's legs free of mud as well as protecting the horse from the heavy stirrups.

▲ Grooms attending a tethered horse. From a 19th-century edition of *Zobyo Monogatari* by Haruta Nobuyoshi. Private collection

▶ Lacquered saddle tree and stirrups Presented to King James I by the Shogun Tokugawa Hidetada.

▶ Iron stirrups decorated with heraldic devices in silver. XXVIB.15

ARMOURS

The armour worn by the *samurai* of the period had evolved specifically for mounted archery. It involved a construction known to modern scholars as lamellar; that is, it was assembled from thousands of overlapping small scales or *lamellae* made from either iron or rawhide. It was a construction that was known in classical antiquity, spreading eastwards through Central Asia to China and Japan. Because only small pieces of iron were needed it was particularly favoured by the nomadic peoples who had only limited metalworking facilities. Japanese scales (*sane*) varied, but most were rectangular, about 5 cm by 3 cm in size, with the top angled off to the right and pierced with 13 holes in two columns. Scales of both iron and rawhide needed to be being heavily lacquered to protect them from the humid climate. To keep the weight of an armour as low as possible, iron scales were only used over the more vulnerable areas and were alternated with rawhide to give a composite - the iron resisting the penetration of an arrow or sword cut, whilst the rawhide sandwiched between absorbed the energy of the blow by being compressed.

Construction of an armour began by lacing the scales into horizontal rows, each scale overlapping its neighbour by half, using leather thongs threaded through the lowest four holes in each column. At each end of the row was a special half scale, added to maintain the thickness. Once all the rows had been assembled they were then laced to each other, overlapping upwards, with strips of deerskin or (later) brightly-coloured silk braid through the remaining holes. At the top of each section of lamellar was a solid iron plate that during this period was covered with decorative stencilled leather held in place by a gilded copper rim.

▲ A partially laced section of armour with the solid plate above. Author's photograph, courtesy of Tokyo National Museum

▼ Row of scales showing stages in lacquering. Author's photograph, courtesy of Tokyo National Museum

In their fully evolved form these armours were known as *o-yoroi* or 'great armours' and comprised a helmet or *kabuto*, a cuirass or *do* – to the lower edge of which were attached pendant flaps over the hips and thighs called *kusazuri* – a pair of shoulder guards or *sode*, armoured sleeves or *kote* and shinguards or *suneate*. Underneath was worn a modified form of a court costume called a *yoroi hitatare* of rich silk brocade consisting of wide pleated trousers tied in just below the knee and jacket with sleeves tied in at the wrist.

▶ Jacket and trousers of brocade for wearing under armour. XXVIA.133

◄ Helmet from an
o-yoroi. xxviA.209

The bowl of the helmet, the *hachi*, was made up from a number of plates of iron, roughly triangular, arranged like the gores of a cap and fastened together with rivets which had large, domed, hollow heads. At the apex was a hole, the *tehen*, surrounded by a decorative rim through which was pulled the excess of a tall soft cap worn in lieu of a helmet lining. On later helmets a permanent fabric lining was fastened to the rim of the bowl, lifting it off the head and thereby reducing concussion when struck. This development obviated the need for a *tehen* and its gilded rim, but both were retained for their decorative qualities. Riveted around the base of the bowl was a continuous strip of metal called the *koshimaki* to which was attached a conical lamellar neck guard or *shikoro* of five rows of scales, the upper rows being extended and turned outwards on either side of the face to form a characteristic feature of most Japanese helmets called the *fukigayeshi*. The original purpose of these wing-like appendages was to protect the face

▲ *Samurai* wearing *waidate* and shinguards. I.303

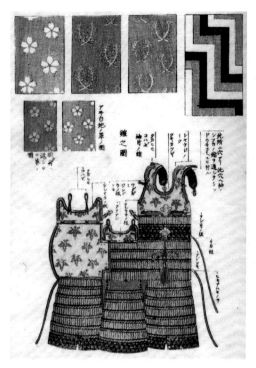

▲ Lamellar section of an *o-yoroi* and stencilled leathers from an 18th-century book on armour, *Gun yo ki* by Ise Sadatake. Private collection

from arrows by the simple expedient of turning the head. On the front of the bowl was a small leather-covered peak, the *mabezashi*, arranged almost vertically so as not to impede the bowstring. At a later date, as the importance of archery declined, the peak moved out from the vertical, becoming almost obscured by an attachment for a pair of horn-like crests called *kuwagata* whilst the *fukigayeshi* degenerated into small tabs.

The *do* of an *o-yoroi* was made in two separate sections: the right side being protected by a solid iron plate called the *waidate* covered in decorative leather that was tied to the body before the rest was put on.

Covering the front, left and back was the *do* proper, made up from four rows of scales called the *nakagawa* with additional rows extending up the back and front, each topped by solid iron plates covered with stencilled deerskin. The rear extension was extended into padded rawhide shoulder straps that fastened to the front plate with cords and toggles. Around the lower edge of the *do* and the *waidate* were four trapezoidal sections of lamellar called the *kusazuri* or 'grass-rubbing' that protected the hips and thighs. When mounted, the *kusazuri* hung over the saddle at the front and back and over the hips and thighs on either side. As a concession to archery, the entire front of the *do* was covered by a sheet of stencilled deerskin to prevent the bowstring catching on the heads of the scales.

Archery demands the use of both hands, so it was not possible for the *samurai* to carry a shield. Instead, two large rectangular sections of lamellar called *sode* were fastened to the shoulder straps of the *do* and hung over the upper arms.

To hold them in position whilst permitting maximum flexibility, a complex of tasselled silk cords connected the *sode* to a large ornamental silk bow hung from a ring attached to the back of the *do*. Early armours left the rest of the arms unprotected but a pair of armoured fabric sleeves called *kote* was soon added. Early *kote* were tied to the body before the *do* and *sode* were put on, and were made of cloth with separate lacquered plates sewn on over the upper and lower arms and over the back of the hand. Later *kote* have the plates connected by mail, *kusari*, of a unique Japanese pattern. These were provided with fastenings at the top that fastened to the shoulder straps of the *do*, thus limiting the weight dragging on the arm. The armour was completed by a pair of tubular plate shinguards, the *suneate*, that were later extended by additional plates over the knee (the most vulnerable part of a horseman's anatomy).

▲ *Sode* for the right side. 16th century. XXVIA.329

▲ Rear of *o-yoroi* showing cords for attaching the sode. I.303

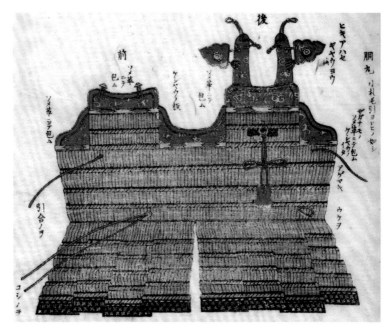

▲ A retainer's *do maru* with *gyoyo* attached to shoulder straps from an 18th-century book on armour, *Gun yo ki* by Ise Sadatake. Private collection

A *samurai*'s retainers, if they were supplied with armour at all, wore a simpler lamellar *do* (a *do maru*) that extended completely around the body, overlapping and fastening under the right arm. Because they had to follow their lord on foot the *kusazuri* were divided into seven or more narrow sections to make walking easier. These retainers were rarely depicted wearing a helmet or defences for the limbs other than a pair of small leaf-shaped plates called *gyoyo* hung on the point of the shoulders from the shoulder straps.

BOWS

For the same reason that horse harnesses had to be made of textiles, the Japanese could not make the superbly efficient composite bows used in most of Asia that involved horn and sinew in their construction. Instead, early bows, *yumi* or *kyo*, were made from hardwood with a strip of bamboo glued to front and back, further blocks of wood being spliced in at the ends to take the nocks for the string. Because bamboo does not take glue well, these bows had to be long to limit the sheer stresses in the glue layers. Most bows are around two metres in length although longer ones are known. Rattan bindings at intervals helped prevent the structure delaminating, whilst coats of lacquer prevented the glue from being softened by the humid climate.

◀ Dismounted *samurai* with his bow. I.303

One peculiarity of these bows was that the grip was positioned towards the lower end, a feature that made it easier to transfer the bow over the horse's neck. During construction the components were glued and tightly bound with cord, the exact shape being adjusted by driving in wedges under the bindings. When complete, the bows curved in the opposite direction to that they assume when strung, thus creating some pre-tension that increased the power when drawn. During later periods the power was increased further by replacing the wood core with strips of bamboo arranged at right angles to the front and back faces, wood being used to fill the gaps on either side of the core and to reinforce the nocks. By varying the thickness of the core, the bowyer could control the draw-weight and hence the power of the bow.

Shorter and weaker bows than those used in battles were made for target practice and for use in shooting galleries. Even smaller bows of

◀ Miniature archery set carried in a palanquin. xxvib.175

▲ A wicker reel for carrying spare bowstrings. Private collection

whalebone or baleen held in a frame with a set of diminutive arrows were carried by nobles in their palanquins in case of attack, their size allowing them to be used in the cramped space. Tiny archery outfits were also made for use in a popular indoor game in which participants shot at a target of silk stretched on a frame. These sets, normally supplied in a fitted box, comprise a small sectional bamboo bow joined by metal mounts and a set of miniature arrows with flat ends that were dipped in ink before shooting so that they left a mark on hitting the target.

ARROWS AND ARROWHEADS

Like the bow, the arrows (*ya*) were also of bamboo, cut in winter and straightened by hand after being heated over glowing charcoal. Once straight, the nodes and outer skin of the bamboo were shaved off and the shafts polished before being sorted so that the positions of the nodes for all the arrows in a set were the same.

The nock for the string was cut just above a node for strength and bound with lacquered silk to reinforce it further. A similar binding above the

▶ Early type of quiver called an *ebira*. XXVIB.157

▼ Set of war arrows in their quiver. XXVIB.29

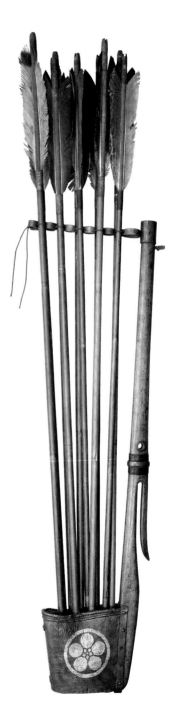

▼ An enclosed quiver, *utsubo*, for use in bad weather. XXVIB.30

head prevented the shaft splitting on hitting the target. Unlike the fletchers of Europe, who used the primary wing feathers for their arrows, the Japanese preferred the tail feathers of either eagles or pheasants. Normally three fletchings were used, glued to the shaft and reinforced with a lacquered binding around the quill at each end. For arrows with a large head, four fletchings were used, two being of eagle in the plane of the head and two of pheasant. For the finest sets of arrows the area between and above the fletchings was gold lacquered. When they were signed, the fletcher would inscribe his name in red lacquer on the binding below the nock.

Arrowheads, *ya no ne*, were of steel, forged with a long tapering tang that fitted into the hollow of the shaft by friction. In cross-section, the heads were usually lozenge- or square-shaped, and were designed to pierce armour. In outline they were likened to and named after the shapes of leaves such as those of the willow. Generally each set contained one arrow with a flat shield-shaped head or *hira ne*, often pierced to reduce the weight. A common theme for the piercing was a cherry blossom but other designs occur.

Tradition has it that these special arrows were used either against high-ranking opponents or to indicate to an opponent that the archer had exhausted his arrow supply. Forked arrowheads in a wide range of sizes were also used. Despite all manners of theories about why these heads were used, such as being used for cutting the rigging of ships or the cords of armours, in reality it was because the width across the points increased the chance of hitting the target. They were called *karimata*, likened to a skein of geese in flight, and were often fitted to a special type of arrow fitted with a bulbous whistle of wood or ivory just under the head. In battle, whistling arrows were used for signalling, but they were also used in religious ceremonies, it being believed that the noise they made would drive away evil spirits.

Like most Asians, the Japanese drew the bow with their right thumb hooked around the string under the arrow with the first one or two fingers pressing on the thumbnail. This practice necessitated the arrow being shot from the right side of the bow as pressure on the thumb tended to pull it straight and rotate the arrow counter clockwise. When practising a special glove was worn with a greatly-enlarged thumb. This was lined with horn and cut with a groove at the first joint for the string. In battle, a pair of ordinary gloves of smoked deerskin was used, enabling the use of the sword and other weapons.

▼ Arrow heads.
XXVIB. 112, 115 and 130

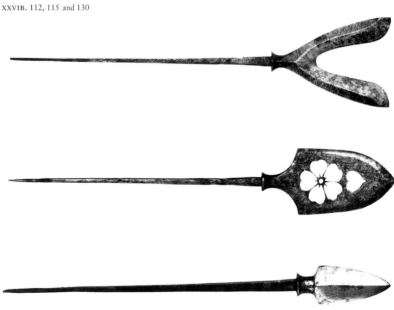

▶ Arrow fitted with a whistle used for signalling. XXVIB.91

► Gloves of smoked leather worn when riding or with armour.
Private collection

▼ Brocade sleeve to protect the clothing when shooting a bow.
Private collection

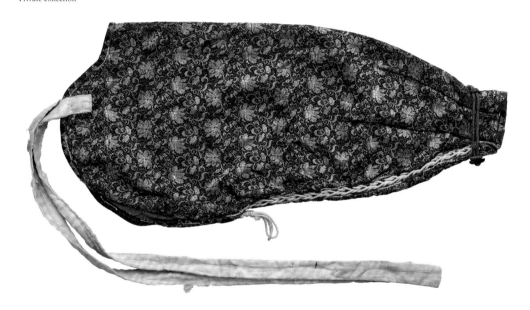

► Glove for archery practice. Private collection

SWORDS

Although the sword is often thought of as the principle weapon of the *samurai*, in battles it was a secondary weapon, only brought into play when the two opposing forces joined. Popular media has given the Japanese sword something of a mythical status and indeed it was a highly efficient weapon in the hands of a master swordsman. Remarkably, it emerged over a millennium ago in a form and of a construction that a hundred thousand later swordsmiths were unable to improve upon. As a consequence sword blades changed little over the centuries. An officer in the Second World War might carry a sword with a blade that was several hundred years old, yet the design would have been barely distinguishable from those made in modern factories.

Swords made during this early period, known as the *koto* or 'old sword' period, can be identified as having characteristics associated with five traditions of swordmaking called the *gokaden*. These traditions were based on the provinces of Yamato, Yamashiro, Bizen, Soshu (or Sagami) and Mino. Each tradition produced blades having features such as its shape, pattern of the hardened edge and so forth that enable an expert to recognise its origins. Inevitably some blades were made by smiths who moved from one area to another and show some mixing of these styles, but in general the differences can be distinguished.

◀ A *samurai* with sword drawn, carrying a *utsubo* from an 18th-century book on armour, *Gun yo ki* by Ise Sadatake.
Private collection

SWORD-MAKING

The Japanese swords differ from those made elsewhere in two important ways. Firstly, the blade was designed to be removed from its mounting and transferred to another as styles changed. This was especially the case in later times when different mounts were worn for different social occasions. The second major difference is the solution devised to solve the problem faced by swordmakers the world over – that steel, despite becoming very hard when rapidly cooled from a high temperature, also becomes very brittle. Steel (that is, iron containing a small percentage of carbon) forms a structure at high temperature that is brittle when cooled rapidly by quenching in water or oil. A blade in this hardened state whilst capable of taking a very sharp edge, is as brittle as glass and would shatter if used in action. In most parts of the world, swords were first fully hardened and then re-heated to a lower temperature, reducing the brittleness at the expense of some loss of hardness – a process known as tempering. Japanese swordsmiths devised an alternative solution that involved hardening only the cutting edge and point, leaving them very hard and brittle but supported and prevented from breaking by the softer and tougher body of the blade. How this was achieved in the distant past is unclear, because nothing was written down until many centuries later. What we can assume is that the process is similar to that used by modern swordsmiths, many of whom have descended in an unbroken line from generations of smiths.

The steel for sword-making was extracted from magnetite, an ore of iron obtained from the beds of rivers. Smelting was carried out by reducing the iron oxide in a rectangular furnace with clay walls using charcoal as the fuel. After a period of about 72 hours, during which time air was constantly blown into the furnace by bellows and additional loads of ore and charcoal were added, a spongy mass of iron, steel and slag called *tamahagane* formed in the base of the furnace. When the firing was judged complete the walls of the furnace were broken down and the white-hot mass or bloom was dragged out and broken into pieces. It was the swordsmiths who had the first choice, selecting those pieces of *tamahagane* that had a high carbon content, the remainder being sold to armourers and blacksmiths.

▲ Forging the *tamahagane* into a block.
© Royal Armouries

▲ A swordsmith and his assistants forging a blade. Author's photograph

When making the various grades of steel used in a blade, the smith needed to assess the carbon content of each piece of *tamahagane*. He did this by heating it and hammering it flat then noting how it broke when cold. Selecting pieces he judged to be rather higher in carbon than the grade of steel needed, he stacked the pieces onto a plate of steel, to which was welded an iron bar that acted as a handle. After wrapping the stack in wet paper to hold it together, it was coated with a slurry of clay to act as a flux and heated to welding temperature in a charcoal-fuelled hearth before hammer-welding the mass into a solid block.

Assisting the smith in this work were assistants wielding large sledgehammers, the smith directing their blows by tapping the block or anvil with a smaller hammer. At this stage the block of steel still contained considerable amounts of slag, was heterogeneous and had too much carbon. It now needed refining. To do this the block was hammered out to twice its length, cut part-way through in the middle, folded over and welded into a block again. During this process some of the slag was hammered out and about 0.03% of the carbon was burnt out. Repeating this process twelve or more times, sometimes hammering it out to twice the width rather than length before welding, eliminated the slag, homogenised the steel and reduced the carbon content to the required level. Throughout this long process, metal was continuously lost through surface oxidation resulting in the loss of two thirds to three-quarters of the starting material.

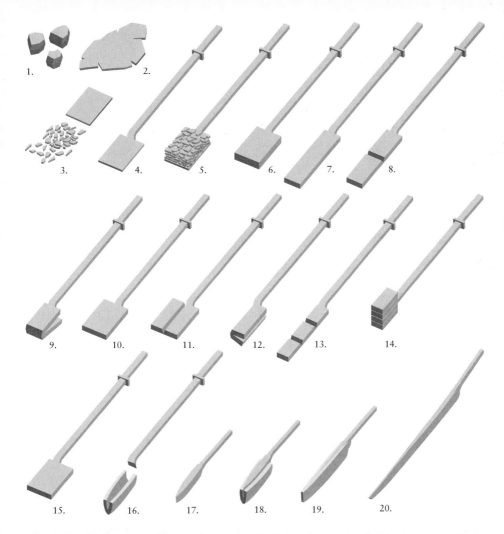

▲ Forging sequence for a sword constructed with a steel outer skin and an iron core. © Royal Armouries

1. Chunks of *tamahagane*.

2. *Tamahagane* flattened into thin sheets.

3. Sheets broken into small wafers.

4. One sheet attached to a handle to form a plate.

5. *Tamahagane* wafers stacked and heated in forge.

6. Heated stack hammered and welded together to form a bar.

7. 8. 9. and 10. Steel bar shaped, folded over and flattened.

11. and 12. Bar folded lengthwise.

13. Bar folded several more times and cut into thirds.

14. and 15. Four pieces of steel from separate forgings are recombined to form a new block which is hammered and folded six or more times to make the skin steel *(kawagane)*.

16. Steel skin folded into 'U' shape.

17. and 18. A length of iron is inserted into the steel and heated in forge.

19. Metal heated, hammered and welded to lengthen until the steel composite is ready to be shaped into the blade blank *(sunobe)*.

20. The blank blade is made shorter and thicker than the final blade to allow for expansion during shaping.

Having produced the various grades of steel, they now had to be combined to produce the blade. For a cheap sword, a block of low carbon steel would be notched and a piece of high carbon steel welded into the groove that would ultimately form the point and cutting edge. A better and more common construction was to form a 'U'-sectioned piece of high carbon steel with one end hammered closed into which a piece of low carbon steel was welded. This produced a final blade with a high carbon steel point, cutting edge and sides with a low carbon steel core. Even more complex were blades having different grades of steel forming the core, edge, sides and back. In all cases, the welding together of the different parts had to be perfect otherwise it would result in weaknesses within the body of the final blade.

▲ The smith dries the clay covered blade before heating to red heat. Author's photograph

Having produced a block with the various steels positioned where they would be needed in the final blade, it was then hammered out into a bar roughly the length and shape of a blade. Great skill was needed in doing this to avoid displacing the position of the steels within the cross-section. With constant reheating and use of a small hammer, the smith would shape the tang, the ridges and point section. Again the constant heating burned off metal and carbon from the surface during this shaping. To prevent this, some smiths welded a sacrificial skin of iron over the block that gradually burned away during the process. Once the smith was satisfied he had done all he could with the hammer, the planes and ridges of the blade were smoothed with a coarse whetstone or a draw-knife.

Having reached this stage the blade was straight and still soft, ready to be given its hard cutting edge and point. This process was started by covering the whole blade in a thin layer of a mixture of clay, charcoal and powdered stone mixed with water. Those areas that were to remain soft were then given a thicker layer of the same mixture together with narrow lines of the mixture crossing the whole blade at various points and at different angles that would create bands of less brittle metal when hardened. These slightly softer lines were designed to stop a crack propagating along the brittle cutting edge should the blade be damaged in action. It was the arrangement

▲ A polisher at work with armourers in the background. Author's photograph

of these lines and the outline of the thicker layer of clay dictating the shape
of the hardened edge that offers clues to the date and origin of a blade. Once
dry, the clay-coated blade was heated in a darkened forge, great care being
taken to achieve a uniform temperature along the whole length of the blade.
When the smith judged by the colour that the blade was at the correct
temperature and evenly heated, it was plunged horizontally in a tank of water.
High-speed photography shows that the blade undergoes remarkable
changes of shape during this quenching. Being coated with only a thin layer
of clay, the cutting edge cools first, contracting as it does so and pulling the
blade into a concave shape. Being covered with thicker clay, the body of the
blade cools more slowly, becoming softer and contracting more, pulling the
blade into its final graceful convex shape. If all had gone well, the smith
would grind off any remaining clay and pass the blade for sharpening and
polishing. If not, the blade could be softened by reheating, and the hardening
process attempted once or twice more.

Unlike western swords, which were sharpened and polished to a bright
finish, Japanese swords were polished in such a way as to show the complex
metallurgy that went into their construction. The polisher began by refining
the planes and lines with a coarse whetstone, using water as a lubricant.
Once satisfied that the shape was what the smith intended, the blade was
worked on a series of ever finer stones to remove the scratches from the
shaping stone. At this stage the hardened edge would be visible, but further

refinement was still needed. Using the ball of the thumb, tiny flakes of special stones were then rubbed on the blade with water. A polisher would need an extensive selection of these flakes, trying them in turn until he found one that gave the effect he was trying to achieve. It was these stones that revealed the grain in the body of the blade, the result of the folding process in forming the skin steel. To finish the polishing process a slightly harder stone was sometimes used to whiten the hardened edge making it stand out more prominently. Finally, on swords with a longitudinal ridge, the area above the ridge and the back were burnished to a bright polish by rubbing with a steel needle.

If he had not done so earlier, the smith would drill a hole in the tang and generally inscribe his name using a chisel. In later periods, smiths also added their place of work, their titles and often the date of manufacture. It is from these inscriptions that scholars have built up a large body of data about the relationships between sword-making groups and the individual smiths within them. Once complete the blade would be provided with the only fitting belonging to it rather than to its mount. This was a tapering collar of soft metal that fitted at the junction of the tang and blade called the *habaki*. Because it butted against shoulders at the edge and back of the blade, the *habaki* transmitted the shock of a blow onto the hilt of the sword. It also had the secondary purpose in that its taper sealed the blade into the mouth of the scabbard when the sword was sheathed.

▶ The swordsmith's name and address on a tang. XXVIS.336

▶ *Right*: The fully polished blade. XXVIS.238

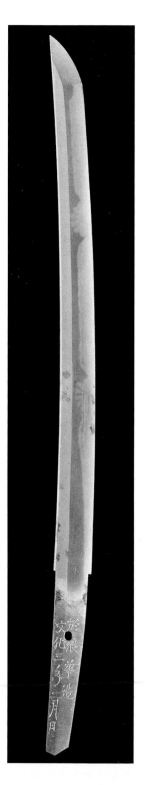

SWORD-MOUNTS

During the Classical era it became normal for the *samurai* to wear two swords: a long sword on the left hip and a short dirk stuck in the belt on the left front.

Wearing two swords became the prerogative of the military class, one always being a long sword with a blade over 60 cm in length. If they wore a sword at all, other classes of society had to be content with a shorter sword.

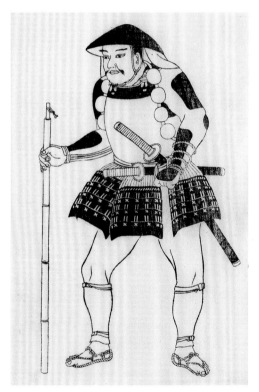

▲ A foot soldier wearing two swords. The round objects around his neck are meals of rice wrapped in cloth. From a 19th-century edition of *Zobyo Monogatari* by Haruta Nobuyoshi. Private collection

◀ A *tanto*. XXVIS.148

All long swords at this period were worn edge downwards in a style of mount called a *tachi*. The scabbard or *saya* was of lacquered magnolia wood whose natural oils helped protect against rusting. Around this were metal mounts consisting of two suspension hangers, an end piece, and various reinforcing rings to prevent splitting. Between the *habaki* and the wooden hilt was a flat guard or *tsuba* with protective washers on each side that not only protected the hand from an opponent's blade but also prevented the user's hand from slipping up onto his own blade. Like the scabbard, the hilt or *tsuka* was of magnolia wood with reinforcing mounts at each end. Hilts were, like the scabbard, made in two halves carved out to exactly fit the tapering tang of the blade. It was this tight fit between the hilt and tang that held the blade solidly in place. To stop the hilt being jarred loose, a tapered peg of bamboo or horn was inserted through the hole in the tang and holes through the hilt. Over the wood of the hilt was pasted a wrapping of *same*, the nodular skin from the back of a species of ray found in the China Sea.

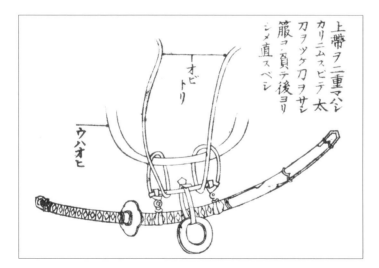

◀ Image showing how a *tachi* was tied to the belt from an 18th-century book on armour, *Gun yo ki* by Ise Sadatake. Private collection

▲ A sword in a *tachi* mount. XXVIS.397

For some swords the rayskin was left exposed, but on most hilts the rayskin was wrapped with silk braid or leather in one of several styles that left diamond-shaped spaces along the length. Trapped under these wrappings on either side, or glued to the *same* of an unwrapped hilt, were small metal ornaments called *menuki* that helped fill out the hilt into the palm of the hand to improve the grip.

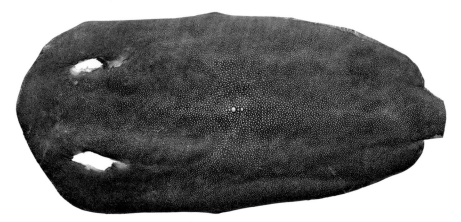

▲ An un-bleached rayskin. Private collection

▲ A *menuki* in the form of a Buddhist divinity. Private collection

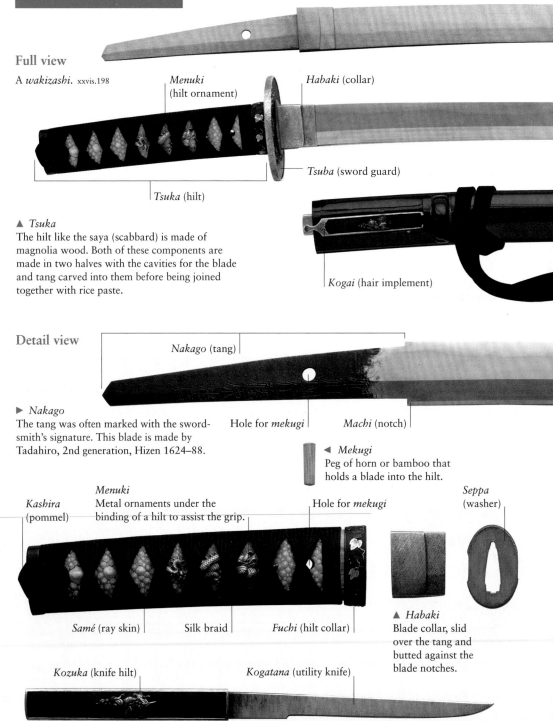

PARTS OF A SWORD

Full view

A *wakizashi.* xxvis.198

Menuki
(hilt ornament)

Habaki (collar)

Tsuba (sword guard)

Tsuka (hilt)

▲ *Tsuka*
The hilt like the saya (scabbard) is made of magnolia wood. Both of these components are made in two halves with the cavities for the blade and tang carved into them before being joined together with rice paste.

Kogai (hair implement)

Detail view

Nakago (tang)

▶ *Nakago*
The tang was often marked with the sword-smith's signature. This blade is made by Tadahiro, 2nd generation, Hizen 1624–88.

Hole for *mekugi*

Machi (notch)

◀ *Mekugi*
Peg of horn or bamboo that holds a blade into the hilt.

Kashira
(pommel)

Menuki
Metal ornaments under the binding of a hilt to assist the grip.

Hole for *mekugi*

Seppa
(washer)

Samé (ray skin)

Silk braid

Fuchi (hilt collar)

▲ *Habaki*
Blade collar, slid over the tang and butted against the blade notches.

Kozuka (knife hilt)

Kogatana (utility knife)

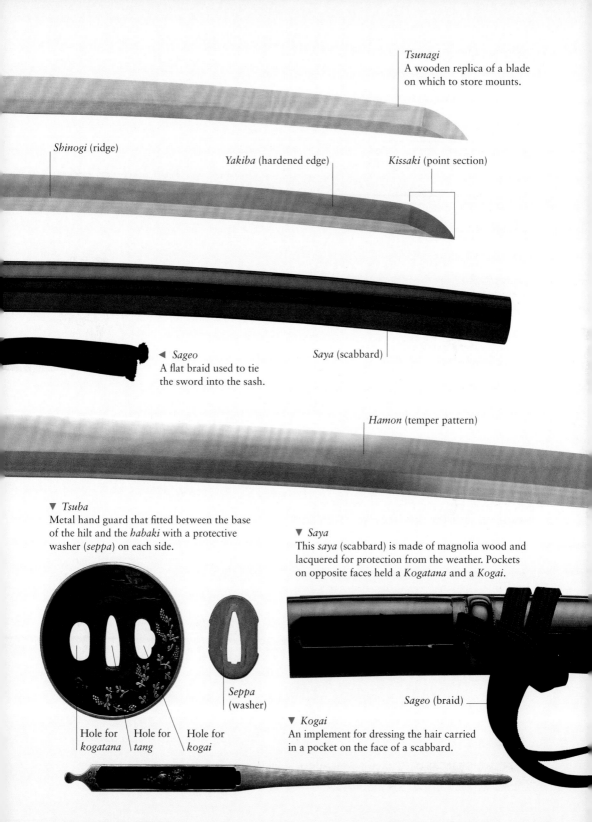

Tsunagi
A wooden replica of a blade
on which to store mounts.

Shinogi (ridge)

Yakiba (hardened edge)

Kissaki (point section)

◄ *Sageo*
A flat braid used to tie
the sword into the sash.

Saya (scabbard)

Hamon (temper pattern)

▼ *Tsuba*
Metal hand guard that fitted between the base
of the hilt and the *habaki* with a protective
washer (*seppa*) on each side.

▼ *Saya*
This *saya* (scabbard) is made of magnolia wood and
lacquered for protection from the weather. Pockets
on opposite faces held a *Kogatana* and a *Kogai*.

Seppa
(washer)

Sageo (braid)

Hole for
kogatana

Hole for
tang

Hole for
kogai

▼ *Kogai*
An implement for dressing the hair carried
in a pocket on the face of a scabbard.

Swordsmiths not only made swords, but also blades for other weapons. Paintings show that the retainers of the *samurai* were generally provided with a sword, but their primary weapon was called a *naginata* or 'mowing-down sword'. At this early date these weapons consist of a long heavy blade about one metre long, curving and swelling at the top and mounted on a shaft just a little longer. Many of the shafts have a spiral wrapping of leather under the lacquer to improve the grip.

Later *naginata* have similar but shorter blades with a thinned back edge and a complex of grooves near the base to lighten them. These were mounted on a proportionally longer shaft fitted with metal mounts and a swelling cord handstop at about the level of the user's shoulder. Far less popular was a type of straight spear called a *kikuchi yari* which had a single-edged, dagger-like blade. Both the *naginata* and *kikuchi yari* blades had long, tapering tangs that fitted into the shafts in a similar to the way the tangs of swords fitted into their hilts.

One famous incident involving the use of the *naginata* took place during the Genpei wars in 1180, on a bridge over the river Uji between Kyoto and Nara. The Minamoto, on the Nara side, had taken the precaution of pulling up the planks of the bridge to prevent the Taira horsemen crossing. Because of a heavy early morning fog, a few Taira urged their horses onto the bridge and had a shock when they plunged into the swirling waters. As the mists cleared, an arrow duel began across the river between the two armies. Amongst the Minamoto forces were a number of Buddhist monks from Miidera monastery, who decided to cross on the beams of the bridge to engage the Taira hand to hand. Leading the group was a monk called Goshin no Tajima. An almost contemporary report continues:

'… then Gochin no Tajima, throwing away the sheath of his long *naginata*, strode forth alone on to the bridge whereupon the Heike (Taira forces) straightaway shot at him fast and furious. Tajima, not at all perturbed, ducking to avoid the higher arrows and leaping up over those that flew low, cut through those that flew straight with his whirring *naginata*, so that even the enemy looked on in admiration. Thus it was that he was dubbed "Tajima the arrow-cutter".'

◄ A foot soldier carrying a *naginata*. From a 19th-century edition of *Zobyo Monogatari* by Haruta Nobuyoshi. Private collection

▼ Fabric cover for the scabbard of a *naginata* with heraldic device. Private collection

▼ An Edo-period *Naginata* with shaft and scabbard. xxvii.219

In the late 13th century, Kublai Khan felt that Japan should be a vassal state of China and sent a series of emissaries demanding that Japan should send tribute to him. After being rebuffed several times, an invasion force was launched in 1274 that landed at Hataka Bay in Kyushu. The assembled *samurai* shouted their challenges and galloped towards the enemy, shooting arrows in their usual way, only to be swallowed up and cut down by ranks of Mongols manoeuvring in unison to commands issued by drumbeats. Not only did the Mongols fight in organised units, they also employed exploding grenades consisting of hollow pottery or iron spheres filled with gunpowder and shrapnel thrown by catapults into the Japanese ranks. The situation was saved for the Japanese when a violent storm sprang up during the night, smashing the Mongol transports and drowning many of the invading troops. Thus was born the legend of the 'Divine Wind', or *kamikaze*.

◀ *Samurai* with a *nagamaki*. © Japan Archive

▼ A *nagamaki* and its mounts. XXVII.284

Following the invasion (and another that ended in a similar way in 1281) mounted archery declined and fighting on foot became more common. The old *o-yoroi* was ill-suited for this purpose and the *samurai* adopted a more refined version of their retainer's *do maru*, adding to it the helmet, shoulder guards and limb defences that they had worn with the *o-yoroi*. The bow continued to be an important weapon in battle but many *samurai* began to use a *naginata* and an allied weapon called a *nagamaki* consisting of a long, heavy sword-like blade on a shaft that was often wrapped with lacquered leather in a similar way to a sword hilt. Designed for use against cavalry, they could be used either to strike the rider as they galloped past or to attack the horse.

▲ Detail showing staff weapons from a painted screen depicting the battle of Nagakute.
© Osaka Castle Museum

▲ Front and rear of a *haramaki* from the Edo period. XXVIA.213

ARMOUR DEVELOPMENT

In 1333 the Emperor Go-Daigo saw an opportunity to wrest power back from an unpopular *shogun* who was favouring his relatives at the expense of those involved in repulsing the Mongol invasions. Go-Daigo was initially encouraged by a noble called Ashikaga Takauji who took the title of *shogun* but who later turned against Go-Daigo and set a new emperor on the throne. Go-Daigo fled south to the Yoshino district of Nara with the imperial regalia and set up a rival court there. There were now two rival centres of power giving rise to a period called the *Nambokucho Jidai*, or the 'Period of the Northern and Southern Courts'. For the next 50 years there was conflict between supporters of the two rivals, which ended in the capitulation of the Southern Court in 1392. During this period armour, although still lamellar, became more refined with smaller scales, elegant colour schemes and applied decorative metalwork in gilded copper.

As the *Nambokucho* era drew to a close, a new style of armour appeared that almost eclipsed the *do maru* in popularity. Because so much fighting was now done with the sword, *naginata* and *nagamaki*, the overlap of the *do* under the right arm could be a hindrance to the sword-arm. This new style was given the name *haramaki*, or 'belly-wrapper', since it opened down the back, the gap being covered by a narrow, separate backplate or *sei ita*.

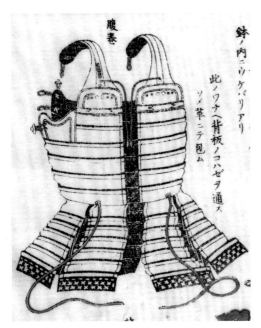

▲ A *haramaki* showing the opening at the back from an 18th-century book on armour, *Gun yo ki* by Ise Sadatake. Private collection

Most *haramaki* were provided with small shoulder guards called *tsubo sode* that tapered towards the bottom and were distinctly curved to fit closely around the upper arm, being far more practical than the large *o-sode* of the past.

Changes were also made to the helmet that had lost the prominent rivets and had the outer edges of each plate turned up into a small flange or *suji*, at this period covered with a gilded rim that connected to a band of ornate, gilded plates encircling the base of the bowl. These *akodanari kabuto*, as they were called, swelled out at the rear and dipped downwards around the *tehen*, being likened to the shape of the newly-imported pumpkin after which they were named. The *shikoro* fitted to the *akoda nari* bowls were less conical than earlier styles, becoming almost horizontal to give the greatest freedom to the arms. The increased use of staff weapons capable of wide sweeping cuts demanded greater protection for the legs. Although the shins were adequately protected by the *suneate*, the lower thighs below the *kusazuri* were vulnerable. Most armours were now provided with a defence for the thighs, either in the form of a pair of baggy shorts with plates sewn on, or a divided apron similarly armoured called a *haidate*.

After so many years of conflict between the two courts, many of the nobles appointed to govern the provinces, the *shugo daimyo*, delegated their responsibilities to minor officials, moving to Kyoto to indulge in luxurious life in the capital. In 1467 a dispute arose over succession to the *shogunate* that led to open warfare between the forces of two of these lords. Other *daimyo* brought their armies from all over the country to join in the fighting. There followed ten years of urban warfare that left the capital a wasteland as around 160,000 men fought themselves to exhaustion. When the war finally petered out, many of the *daimyo*, their troops decimated and exhausted, found they had been usurped by those they had left in charge of their estates. Noble families who had held positions of power for centuries sank into oblivion whilst the status of minor families rose – a phenomena called *gekoku jo* or 'those below overthrowing those above'.

◀ A *suji bachi*.
XXVIA.64

◄ Armour of the late
16th century with
akodanari helmet,
presented to King
James I of England.
XXVIA.1

THE COUNTRY AT WAR (1467 – 1543)

With the *shogunate* weakened and unable to keep the peace, the strictly-ordered society disintegrated and conflicts broke out all over the country. Lower-class *samurai*, peasants and monks united to form armies called *ikki* which conquered territory and in some cases even set up local governments. It was the prelude to a prolonged period of widespread civil wars that was to last some 150 years – a terrible period now known as the *Sengoku Jidai*, or the 'Age of the Country at War'. Many of the original *shugo daimyo* lost their lands, being replaced by others who became known as the *sengoku daimyo* or more usually just *daimyo*, meaning 'great landowners'; their estates or territories being known as *han*. From this time onwards, Japan's political and social structure was to be dominated by the *daimyo* who theoretically owed their allegiance to the *shogun* and through him to the emperor, but sometimes ignored both.

◄ *Opposite*: Detail of a red lacquered *hineno zunari kabuto*.
XXVIA.224

◄ Spearmen – the one on the right has looted swords and a trophy head. From a 19th-century edition of *Zobyo Monogatari* by Haruta Nobuyoshi.
Private collection

One essential difference between the nobles of the past and the new *daimyo*, many of whom had fought their way up from quite lowly positions, was that they were prepared to recruit the lower classes into their armies. For the first time, farmers and peasants joined infantry units called *ashigaru* ('light feet'), motivated primarily by the potential for bettering their lot by looting. The commanders of these untrained troops were faced with the problem of how best to use them.

There was little point in issuing them with the traditional weapons of the *samurai* that could take years of practice to master as well as being prohibitively expensive. The answer lay in the simple spear or *yari*, which in desperate circumstances might be nothing more than a length of bamboo with the end cut off at an angle. Spear heads were relatively cheap to produce and the shafts could be made by any competent woodworker. Issued with a spear and supplied with some form of sword, often made up from damaged or worn out blades, the *ashigaru* units became a force to be reckoned with. These troops had another advantage that only became apparent later. Whereas most *samurai* still clung to remnants of their fighting tradition, acting independently with their retainers, the *ashigaru* could be controlled as units under the command of a single officer.

Once the *daimyo* had seen the potential of the *ashigaru* it became apparent that they had to be properly equipped. By the 16th century most *ashigaru* were issued with simple armours, usually decorated with the heraldry of their lord. Because all this equipment was provided by their lord, it was described with the prefix *okashi-* or 'honorably lent'.

SPEARS

Although there were variations, most spears had a parallel-sided head with a lozenge or triangular cross-section. Like sword blades, spearheads were forged with a long tapering tang that fitted to a cavity cut in the top of the shaft, being retained there by a bamboo peg through a hole in the shaft and tang. At the top of the shaft, made from red oak, was a metal sleeve to stop the wood splitting, with further reinforcing rings around the part of the shaft that had been split to carve out the cavity. Most ordinary spears had the top of the shaft lacquered in some way, the remainder being plain polished wood. A favourite finish was to embed small pieces of mother-of-pearl in the lacquer and then polish it smooth. At about the level of the user's shoulder was a bulbous wrapping of cord around the shaft that acted as a handstop, whilst at the butt of the shaft was an iron shoe. Like all bladed weapons in Japan, spears were equipped with scabbards. Made of lacquered wood,

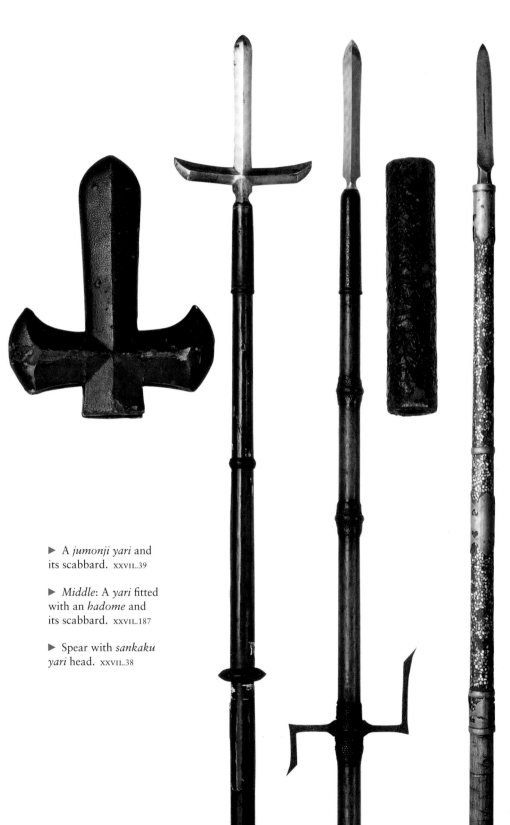

▶ A *jumonji yari* and its scabbard. XXVII.39

▶ *Middle*: A *yari* fitted with an *hadome* and its scabbard. XXVII.187

▶ Spear with *sankaku yari* head. XXVII.38

some were simply utilitarian but many were of fanciful shapes, colours and textures with a heraldic significance.

Many spears had shafts about two metres long, but as the *Sengoku jidai* wore on spears began to lengthen – not unlike the pikes of Europe – as a defence against cavalry. One *daimyo* of the era, Oda Nobunaga, armed some of his men with *yari* some 5.5 metres in length. Another development that appeared was a cross-bar of iron just above the handstop called a *hadome*. This could be used for parrying an opponent's blade, as the name implies, or for hooking behind an opponent's leg or neck and pulling them over.

Whilst simple straight spear blades were by far the most common, there were variants. Very rarely a blade might be leaf-shaped, or (more frequently) had one or two side blades. That with only one side blade, positioned at a right angle to the base of the main blade, was called a *hoko*. Those with two blades were called *jumonji yari* due to the fact that they resembled the cross-shaped character for the numeral 10 (十).

ARMOUR

The appearance of spears and the protracted campaigns that were a feature of this chaotic period led to profound changes to the armour of the *samurai*. The old lamellar armour, with its large quantities of silk lacing, was found to have disadvantages when it was worn day after day on prolonged campaigns. When wet, the lacing absorbed so much water it almost doubled the weight; it was also difficult to clean or to dry out in a camp, and the numerous crevices between the scales could harbour vermin. One expedient that was unsuccessfully tried was to cover the entire *do* and its lacing in thin leather, a strategy that reduced flexibility and limited mobility. A more successful solution was to make the iron scales wider and assemble them with only the minimum of overlap, lacing them onto a strip of thick leather to hold them together. When this structure was wrapped in thin leather and lacquered, it was relatively light, flexible and waterproof. This *iyozane* construction, as it was called, could be pierced for only the minimum amount of lacing needed to hold the armour together. Generally the lacing was arranged in pairs, spaced out along the row, a style called *sugake odoshi* or 'simple hang lacing', as opposed to the traditional *kebiki odoshi* or 'hair spread all over lacing' used previously.

Whereas previous armours had to defend mainly against cuts from swords, *naginata* or the relatively low-energy impact of arrows, it now had to defend against the thrust of spears as well. Both *haramaki* and *do maru* had evolved to give the wearer the greatest freedom of movement when using

▲ Shoulder guards laced in *kebiki* style (left) and *sugake* style (right). Private collection

a sword or staff weapon. One feature designed to achieve this was the *kusazuri* that was divided into ten or more sections so as not to impede movement of the hips and legs. Although the multiple sections of lamellar still gave protection against cuts, the large number of gaps between them became an easy target for a spearman. Consequently the number of sections of *gessan*, as these were now known, was reduced to six or seven.

An even more profound change was to increase the number of rows of scales in the *nakagawa* from four to five, giving greater protection to the lower abdomen and allowing the *do* to sit on the hips, relieving some of the weight off the shoulders. Another vulnerable area was the upper chest, originally protected by a *mune ita* that had a flat upper edge with rounded projections at each end for the shoulder strap fastenings. This now changed in shape to fit closer to the neck, and gained a rolled-out upper edge to deflect a spear point away from the throat.

Although these changes went a long way towards increasing the utility of armours, the real answer lay in abandoning lamellar construction and making armour from rawhide plates. This did not involve any significant change in technology, and many armours were constructed entirely of this material. When the plates were more or less flat, an iron bar was laced to the back side before lacquer was applied. This helped to prevent warping.

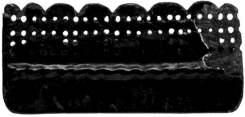

▲ Outside and inside of rawhide plate from a *gessan* showing the stiffening bar. The outer surface modelled in lacquer to look like *iyozane*. Unused holes show the rawhide has been recycled.
Private collection

◄ A face mask of lacquered rawhide.
Private collection

The manufacture of complex shapes such as helmet bowls and face masks involved stretching and nailing the wet hide over a wooden block that had been carved to the shape required. X-rays of rawhide masks carried out at the Royal Armouries show that additional nails were used to force the hide into concave areas. As the hide dried, it shrank and retained the shape of the block; any excess hide was then trimmed off before lacquering. For helmet bowls and other parts of the armour that needed maximum resistance, multiple layers of hide were glued or sewn together to give sufficient thickness. These rawhide armours were almost as effective as those made of iron, but were considerably lighter in weight and found favour with elderly *samurai*.

◀ *Haramaki* of
mogami construction
presented to King
Philip II of Spain
in 1585. XXVIA.2

Clearly, neither hide nor iron plate armours had the flexibility in the *nakagawa* to open out for putting on, so the obvious solution was to divide the horizontal plates into sections joined by hinges. Most iron armours have the horizontal strips of plate divided into five sections: front, left side, back and two half plates under the right arm, all joined by hinges. This arrangement made opening the armour easy and also had the benefit of being assembled from relatively small pieces of iron. Any *do* in which each plate had a number of small individual hinges on each plate are described as being of *mogami* construction.

Although effective, the small hinges were rather fragile and were soon replaced by more robust hinges that extended down all five rows in the *nakagawa*. By making the pins of these hinges removable, the *do* could be dismantled into five separate sections making it easier to repair or pack for storage and transport. Any *do* that can be divided into five separate sections is known as a *go mai do* ('five plate body'). An alternative was to use only one hinge under the left arm, allowing the *do* be divided into two pieces – a *ni mai do*.

Many who appreciated the utility of plate armours yet wanted to retain the appearance of traditional lamellar armour had armours made with false scales. To create this effect, armourers serrated the upper edge of the

◀ A *go mai do* of plate in a style known as a *yukinoshita do* popular in the Sendai region. XXVIA.100

plates like a row of scale heads and drilled it with holes for *kebiki* lacing. To complete the deception, the visible surface of the plate was modelled with lacquer in a series of ridges that resembled a row of scales. This effect was known as *kiritsuke kozane* or *kiritsuke iyozane* ('cut out and stuck on scales').

Samurai individualised the *do* of their armour so they stood out on the battlefield by using coloured lacquer or in other ways. Simplest were *ni mai do*, made up from plain horizontal plates (*yoko hagi okegawa do*), or vertical plates (*tate hagi okegawa do*). It was *do* of these constructions that were issued to *ashigaru*, but higher-quality versions were also worn by *samurai*. Other *do* were covered in filler and lacquered smooth, giving the appearance of being made from a single plate. These were called *hotoke do*, alluding to the Buddha and meaning 'unblemished'. Others had cross-knots of silk or leather fastening the plates together, a style called *hishinui do*, or with ornate soft metal rivets giving a *byo toji do*.

▲ An *ashigaru* putting on his armour. From a 19th-century edition of *Zobyo Monogatari* by Haruta Nobuyoshi. Private collection

▶ A *ni mai do* of *kiritsuke kozane*.
XXVIA.45

HELMETS

Improvements in metalworking enabled larger sheets of iron to be produced
that in turn allowed armours to devise new forms of helmet. Most popular
were *zunari kabuto* or 'head-shaped helmets', made with a wide plate running
from front to back over the top of the head with a plate either side joining it
to a wide *koshimaki*. There were two styles of this helmet. The first type,
favoured by Hosokawa Lord of Etchu and hence
called an *etchu zunari kabuto*, had the top plate
overlap a browplate that flared out into a wide
concave peak with a flat lower edge. The second
type devised by a *samurai* called Hineno
Hironari and called a *hineno zunari kabuto* had
the top plate overlapped by the browplate that
flared out into a concave peak turned down at
each side over the temples. Fitted to these
helmets were two styles of close-fitting neck
guards, the *etchu zunari shikoro* having a
horizontal lower edge, the *hineno shikoro* being
arched over the shoulders and extending down
at the back to protect the neck.

◀▲ A red lacquered
hineno zunari kabuto
made for the Ii family.
XXVIA.224

Other simple helmets were made by riveting around the edges of two shaped plates and opening them out at the bottom. Those shaped like a court cap were called *eboshi nari kabuto*; those rising to a blunt point were likened to a peach and called *momo nari kabuto*. Like the rest of the armour, these helmets could be lacquered in all manner of finishes, some of the *zunari* helmets being covered in bear bristles embedded in lacquer and dressed to resemble various hairstyles. Others took this idea of distinctive helmets further by having elaborate superstructures of lacquered wood, leather and paper added to simple *zunari* helmets. The models chosen for these *harikake kabuto* varied from animal heads and inanimate objects to abstract shapes. One famous warrior called Kato Kiyomasa wore a silver lacquered court cap almost a metre in height. Another favourite were helmets modelled on a large spreading scallop shell. All of these novelty helmets are generically known as *kawari kabuto* or 'novel helmets'.

◄ *Harikake kabuto* modelled with a silver lacquered scallop shell.
XXVIA.89

A new addition that appeared for almost all armours was some form of face mask from which hung a short laced section of plates to protect the throat. By far the most popular at this period was an abbreviated mask called a *hanbo*, covering only the chin and cheeks so as not to limit vision or interfere with breathing. Whilst it gave some protection to the face, hooks and standing posts on the cheeks and chin enabled the helmet cord to be tied more securely to the mask than onto the face itself. Also available were masks that covered the entire face below the eyes. These should strictly be called a *me no shita bo* or 'face below the eyes', but are generally referred to as a *menpo*. When embossed with wrinkles and fitted with teeth and a moustache to give them an intimidating appearance, they were called *reisei men* or 'fierce face'. Strangely, high-ranking warriors tended to wear *menpo* that had no teeth and a gentle, dignified expression.

In previous centuries, the majority of helmets had an ornate 'U'-shaped socket fastened over the peak that carried a pair of horn-like crests called *kuwagata*; at a later date these also sported a straight Buddhist sword blade between the crests. During the era of the civil wars the *samurai* wanted to be seen doing brave deeds on the battlefield due to the potential rewards that would follow, and therefore sought to be as distinctive as possible. One way of doing this was to adorn the helmet with elaborate crests. These were attached by simple hooks riveted to the bowl. Of necessity crests had to be light and many were little more than silhouettes of gilded copper or gold lacquered rawhide but some were elaborate lacquered three-dimensional wooden carvings.

▶ Russet armour showing how the helmet ties to the mask. Private collection

◀ A collapsible helmet
likened to a folding
lantern with its gilded
crest. Private collection

▶ A light folding
helmet with yak-hair
over an armoured
cape. XXVIA.93

The subject matter might be heraldic, depictions of animals, man-made objects, plant forms or of religious significance. Others wore helmets covered by wigs of yak- or horsehair. Algernon Mitford, a secretary at the British Legation in the mid-19th century, witnessed the *shogun's* last entry into Osaka castle and describes how he was followed by:

'... warriors dressed in the old armour of the country, carrying spears, bows and arrows, falchions curiously shaped, with sword and dirk who looked as if they had stepped out of some old pictures of the Gempei wars in the Middle Ages. Their *jinbaori*, not unlike herald's tabards, were as many coloured as Joseph's coat. Hideous masks of lacquer and iron, fringed with portentous whiskers and mustachios, crested helmets with wigs from which long streamers of horse-hair floated to their waists, might strike terror into any enemy. They looked like the hobgoblins of a nightmare.'

Jinbaori

The *jinbaori* mentioned by Mitford was a kind of sleeveless surcoat worn over the armour, especially when travelling. Many are of imported woollen cloth dyed in bright primary colours with the wearer's heraldry displayed below the collar on the back, and sometimes bold stylised designs in contrasting colours. Most have the edges of the front opening turned outwards and faced with rich brocade.

▶ *Jinbaori* of brocade lined with imported European cloth. Author's photograph, courtesy of Watanabe Museum

IDENTIFICATION

Another development that enabled commanders to follow the progress of their troops, as well as to identify individuals, was the practice of wearing a flag called a *hata sashimono* flown from a pole attached to the backplate.

For this purpose most armours of the era have a bracket attached to the backplate at the level of the shoulder blades and a socket at the waist. The design of these flags might be heraldic but just as often were adorned by stripes or blocks of colour. A painted screen depicting the battle of Nagakute (1584) shows many of the *samurai* wearing *sashimono* consisting of three-dimensional gilded objects on poles instead of flags. Among the subjects for these devices are fish, chess pieces, baskets, windmills and similar objects. It is possible that the weather on that occasion was windy, making *hata sashimono* impractical. The commanders too employed flags, banners and other insignia, often of enormous size, to indicate their positions overlooking the battlefield. Tall, narrow flags called *nobori* would flutter alongside gilded standards such as fans or gourds acting as rallying, or reference, points for the troops in the chaos of a battle.

▲ The fittings for a *sashimono* on the back of an armour. XXVIA.288

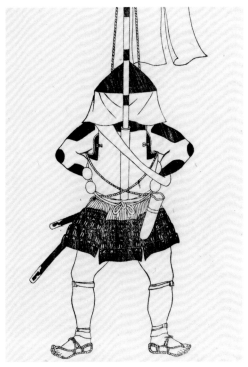

▲ An *ashigaru* carrying a *nobori* attached to his backplate. From a 19th-century edition of *Zobyo Monogatari* by Haruta Nobuyoshi. Private collection

► Detail from a painted screen depicting the battle of Nagakute showing *sashimono* being worn with *nobori* in the background. © Osaka Castle Museum

SWORD DEVELOPMENT

Whilst cavalry continued to play a role in many armies, now armed with swords and spears rather than bows, much of the fighting was on foot for which the traditional *tachi* mount was less useful. Whilst running it swung on its hangers, banging against the body and making the hilt tricky to access. In other words the hilt was never in the same place. A long blade, necessary on horseback to reach an opponent, was something of a hindrance when used in a close press of troops. A replacement form of mounting was found in the swords that had been issued to the *ashigaru*. This style of mounting, whilst similar to the *tachi*, had no hangers and the sword was instead thrust through the belt on the left hip, with the edge uppermost. This had the advantage that the hilt was always in the same position allowing a rapid draw if required. Swords mounted in this way were known as *uchi gatana* and for a while were worn as a supplement to the *tachi*, but gradually replaced it. From this time onwards, although *tachi* remained as the proper wear when in armour or when attending court, a descendant of the *uchi gatana* became more usual.

◄ A portrait of Honda Tadakatsu (1548-1610) wearing a *tachi*, *uchigatana* and a dirk.

© Tachisaka Shrine

THE ARRIVAL OF THE GUN (1543 – 1603)

In 1543 two important events occurred that were ultimately to break the stalemate of the civil wars. One was the birth of a child, the son of the Daimyo of Mikawa, who was given the name of Matsudaira Takachiyo; the other was the arrival of a Chinese ship that took shelter off the island of Tanegashima at the southern tip of Kyushu. On board the ship were three Portuguese merchant adventurers who carried guns. News of the arrival of foreigners and their new wonder-weapon reached the local *daimyo*, Tokitaka, who invited the Portuguese to demonstrate their firepower. After some bargaining, Tokitaka bought one of the guns and ordered his swordsmith to make copies. Another of his staff was given instructions on the making of gunpowder from a member of the ship's crew. Despite the difficulty of making the screwed breechplug, the swordsmith finally managed to make copies of the gun that Tokitaka gave as presents to his relatives on the mainland. Within a couple of decades, knowledge of the gun had spread so rapidly throughout the country that a *daimyo* on Honshu, Oda Nobuhide, could visit his intended father-in-law with a guard that contained 500 gunners.

▲ Screen depicting Portuguese merchants arriving in Japan. © Nikko Toshogu Shrine

◀ *Opposite*: Detail of a *teppo*. XXVIF.52

The guns borne by these merchants were not the first to be seen in Japan. There are literary records that describe a Chinese gun arriving in Osaka in 1510, but no details about it survive. The guns brought by the Portuguese in 1543 were not European in origin but had been made in Goa, India. During the same year the Chinese gun reached Osaka, the Portuguese had established a base in Goa, taking over an existing arsenal and staffing it with German overseers to make guns for their East Asian operations. The guns they produced were technically 'snapping matchlocks': they were fired using a length of smouldering cord, or match, held in the jaws of a pivoting arm called the serpentine that was operated by a spring. Firing the gun involved loading the barrel with gunpowder and ball, and adding a small amount of priming powder to a pan on the side of the barrel that connected to the main charge. This pan was then closed by a cover to prevent accidental discharge and protect the priming from wind and rain. When ready to fire, the serpentine was pulled upwards, away from the pan and held by a catch operated by the trigger. Just before firing, the match was fitted to the serpentine, the gun sighted and the pan cover opened before pulling the trigger. This enabled the spring to snap the serpentine down into the pan, thus igniting the priming powder which in turn ignited the main charge.

The copies of these guns made in Japan were similar in size to a musket, with barrels about 120 cm long and a bore around 16 mm diameter. Smaller, shorter guns, called *bajo zutsu* or 'horsemen's guns', and large bore guns

▼ A *teppo* that has been lacquered, probably as a wedding gift, showing the snapping mechanism.
XXVIF.52

▲ A *kakae o zutsu*, the lock is missing. xxvif.209

▼ Detail of the barrel of a *kakae o zutsu* with the heraldry of the Tokugawa family and the name of the gun: 'Abyss'. xxvif.209

(*kakae o zutsu*) were also made. Some of the latter weighed as much as 11 kg and were mainly used to attack gates and similar fortifications.

All types of gun were stocked in oak to the muzzle and fitted with brass furniture that was not only corrosion-resistant but could be cast in almost finished condition. Unlike the Goan gunmakers, the Japanese were never comfortable making screw threads, preferring to use tapered pins rather than screws to hold the various parts of the lock together and to hold it into the stock. There was no butt as such: the stock ended in a pistol-grip that was held against the right cheek when shooting.

Guns were known by a variety of names: *tanegashima* (after their place of arrival), *teppo* (using the characters for 'fire' and 'iron'), or more properly *hi nawa ju*, that uses the characters 'fire', 'rope' and 'tube'. Almost from the start, guns were made in standard bore sizes simplifying the provisioning of ammunition. The system used involved the weight of a lead ball measured in *momme* that exactly fitted the barrel (one *momme* being 3.75 g). Typical sizes were:

Momme	4	5	6	8	10	20	30	100	150	200
Diameter (mm)	13.8	14.9	15.8	17.4	18.7	23.2	26.4	40.3	45.2	47.8

Many *han* developed their own individual style of gun, but large-scale production was concentrated in centres such as Sakai, near Osaka and Kunitomo on the northern shore of Lake Biwa in central Japan. In both these centres, separate workshops specialised in one part of the manufacturing process, with batches of parts passed from one shop to another to complete the order. The gunmakers of Kunitomo specialised in munitions guns that were occasionally of doubtful quality, being given the name *udon ju* or 'noodle guns' because their barrels tended to flex on firing. Sakai became renowned for guns that were elaborately decorated with brass inlays in the stocks, some with bought-in barrels that were taken to Sakai for finishing.

▲ *Ashigaru* gunner. From a 19th-century edition of *Zobyo Monogatari* by Haruta Nobuyoshi. Private collection

   Gun barrels were forged by bending a strip of iron into a 'U'-section, then hammering it into a tube and welding along the seam around a mandrel (a tapered, rusted, iron rod coated with lime or similar substance that prevents the tube sticking to it). Top quality barrels had further strips of iron welded in a spiral around the tube to improve the resistance to breech pressures. Once forged and the mandrel removed, the rough tube was bored out with a square-sectioned cutter, the front edges removing excess metal and the edges of the cutter scraping the bore smooth. At the breech end, a screwed plug called the *bisen* was fitted before the sights and the pan were added by dovetails and brazing. Many surviving guns have the barrels

▼ A bullet mould. XXVIF.225

decorated with inlay or overlay in silver, gold and other metals. Much of this work was done at a later date when guns had become symbols of rank and wealth rather than practical weapons.

Gunners carried a length of match, made from hemp or bamboo fibre, carried in a coil around the left wrist of a length sufficient for about eight hours. Gunpowder for the main charge and finer-grained powder for the priming could be carried in flasks of lacquered leather or wood, the caps acting as a measure. In battles, the troops were issued with cartridges consisting of cardboard or bamboo tubes that held a measure of powder and a ball to simplify loading. These cartridges were carried in a box of folded, lacquered leather worn on the right hip, examples of which were exhibited in Paris in the 19th century that apparently inspired Louis Vuitton's luggage designs.

▲ A bib worn over armour or clothing, to protect from sparks and soot when shooting a gun.
XXVIF.229

▶ A cartridge case.
Private collection

▲ A powder flask
made from bamboo.
Private collection

◀ A lacquered powder flask.
Detail shows the cap
removed. XXVIF.117

In 1575 the gun proved its value in a battle involving two of Japan's most
forward-thinking *daimyo*, near the castle at Nagashino in the province of
Mikawa. The commander of the castle, Okudaira Sadamasa, was a vassal of
the Daimyo of Mikawa, the now grown Matsudaira Takachiyo who had
changed his name to Tokugawa Ieyasu. Laying siege was Takeda Katsuyori
who claimed that the castle was threatening his supply lines. Ieyasu, still a
relatively minor figure, had concerns about taking on such a powerful enemy
whose army was renowned for its formidable cavalry. Ieyasu sent a request

for help to Oda Nobunaga, Daimyo of Owari and son of the above-mentioned Oda Nobuhide. Some 38,000 troops, about a thousand of whom were armed with guns, were assembled to relieve the castle. The site chosen for the actual battle was a small plain a few miles distant from the castle where palisades and embankments were thrown up in front of a wooded hillside. Parallel to these defences, about 50 metres away, was a small, deep stream that – it was hoped – would slow the charge of the horsemen. Katsuyori detached 12,000 men, leaving 3,000 to keep the castle garrison pinned down, confident that the poor weather would lessen the effect of the gunners. Expecting the usual shock effect that his charging horsemen had on his opponents, Katsuyori ordered them to charge. However, he had underestimated the effect of the stream, which slowed the horses and gave the gunners almost static targets at close range. Some gunners were positioned in front of the palisades as bait, whilst behind were earthworks with three steps upon which were positioned three ranks of gunners who fired in rotation. Those horsemen who did reach the palisades were funnelled into gaps by *ashigaru* spearmen, behind which were killing zones where others attacked their flanks. Charge after charge was defeated and, by the afternoon, Katsuyori retreated with only a remnant of his army. In total, some 2,000 or more Takeda men were dead, mainly at the hands of the *ashigaru*.

With the Takeda defeated, Oda Nobunaga felt free to continue the programme of expansion he had started years before. In this he was aided by his generals, and in particular by Hashiba Hideyoshi, a peasant who had risen by sheer ability. Unlike other *daimyo* who simply conquered territory, Nobunaga moved into those provinces that would ensure supplies to maintain his armies. In 1582, prior to yet another phase of expansion, Nobunaga decided to rest in a temple in Kyoto whilst his generals moved against various strongholds. Hashiba Hideyoshi was ordered to lay siege to Takamatsu castle, a Mori family stronghold in Bitchu province. Another general, Akechi Mitsuhide, was ordered to assist Hideyoshi but for reasons that are still in doubt moved on Kyoto, attacking the temple in which Nobunaga was staying. Having only his personal guards and being completely outnumbered, Nobunaga committed suicide and set fire to the building to prevent his head being taken. Another contingent of Mitsuhide's forces attacked a second temple where Nobunaga's son was staying, killing him. As soon as Hideyoshi heard of the attack, he made a truce with the Mori and raced to Kyoto, tracking down and killing Mitsuhide a few days later. Ignoring the claims of another of Nobunaga's sons and other Oda generals, Hashiba Hideyoshi fought for and won command of the Oda army, continuing the programme of conquest begun by Nobunaga. Tokugawa Ieyasu initially moved against Hideyoshi but eventually accepted he had no alternative but to declare himself a vassal. As a reward he was offered the fertile Kanto plain in place of his ancestral mountainous provinces. He chose as his capital the small fishing village of Edo, building a castle and strengthening his forces. Meanwhile, Hideyoshi continued the expansion began by Nobunaga, finally uniting the country and building a vast castle in Osaka. Being born a peasant meant he could not take the title of *shogun*, instead he had himself adopted into a noble family and was granted the title of Regent and given the name Toyotomi by the Emperor Go-Yozei.

With Japan essentially at peace, Hideyoshi faced a number of problems, not least that of being in control of a country awash with weapons and teeming with fighting men who knew no other life but war. An additional problem was that many of the vassals of defeated lords had not only lost their incomes but were also too proud to work. They become *ronin* ('wave men') who eked out a living any way they could, often becoming bandits. Even the *ashigaru* posed a challenge. Having tasted life beyond the confines of farming, they were reluctant to return to their former stations.

▼ The battle of Nagashino as depicted on a screen. © Osaka Castle Museum

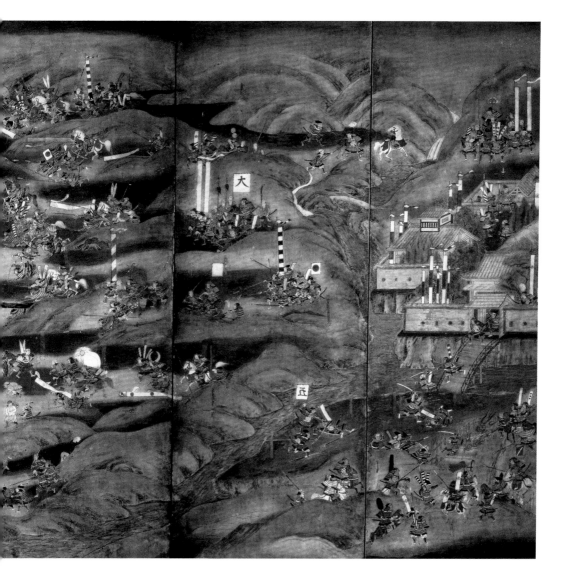

One of Hideyoshi's first move was to disarm as much of the country as he could, sending inspectors around the country confiscating weapons from all who were not of *samurai* class, ostensibly to erect a vast statue of the Buddha in celebration of the peace. He solved the problem of what to do about the *samurai* by giving them some fighting to do, but not on Japanese soil. In 1592 he realised a long-held ambition and organised an expedition to conquer China by way of Korea. A large invasion force led by senior *daimyo* was dispatched and soon occupied Seoul. Within four months they had conquered most of Korea, before the Chinese dispatched a vast army to block their route into Manchuria. Despite being a military success this invasion, and a second attempt in 1598, failed because of the Korean navy's disruption of supply lines.

▲ *Ashigaru* shooting in rain with protective covers over the gun locks. 1.160

During the second Korean invasion Hideyoshi died, leaving his young son Hideyori in the care of both civil and military guardians. One of the latter was Tokugawa Ieyasu who was soon in dispute with others and withdrew from Osaka back to Edo. Accompanying him was the pilot of a Dutch ship, the remnant of a Dutch fleet that had left Rotterdam in 1598. The pilot was an Englishman, Will Adams, who was seen by Ieyasu as a useful source of information and, being a Protestant, a counter to the Catholics. Adams was never allowed to leave Japan, being made a *samurai* by Ieyasu under the name of Miura Anjin and being given estates and a Japanese wife.

With the guardians of Toyotomi Hideyori at loggerheads, the country polarised into two great groups: that in the east was led by Tokugawa Ieyasu; that in the west by Ishida Mitsunari, one of the civil guardians of Hideyori. The crisis-point came in 1600 when the two forces met on a wet foggy morning at a cross-roads in the village of Seki ga Hara. In all some 200,000 men took the field with parts of both armies failing to arrive because of minor skirmishes elsewhere. During the battle, six *daimyo* in the western army either defected or stood their ground, resulting in the defeat of Mitsunari and victory for Tokugawa Ieyasu.

THE EDO PERIOD (1603 – 1853)

Following his victory at Seki ga Hara, Ieyasu set about consolidating his position, executing some opponents and stripping both land and title from others that had opposed him. Some of the confiscated lands were given to supporters, but Ieyasu also gained considerably, becoming the richest *daimyo* in the country. Within three years he had been appointed *shogun*, establishing a regime that was to last some 250 years.

His castle town of Edo grew rapidly as craftsmen and merchants flocked to the new centre of power, becoming within a short time the largest city in the world.

◀ *Opposite*: Detail of a gold lacquered Edo-period armour.
XXVIA.247

◀ Portrait of Tokugawa Ieyasu.
© Nikko Toshogu Shrine

After only three years as *shogun*, Ieyasu retired in favour of his son
Tokugawa Hidetada but nevertheless continued to hold onto much of his
power from his retirement home in Sumpu (now Shizuoka). Although there
was a brief period of peace, the young Toyotomi Hideyori, still living in his
father's castle in Osaka, was reaching maturity and gaining support from
those bearing a grudge against the Tokugawa for their defeat at Seki ga Hara.
The Spanish Catholics too were becoming a concern for the *shogun*: they
tended to support the Toyotomi cause and were suspected of interfering in
Japan's politics.

Ieyasu and Hidetada finally acted, banning Christianity from their
territories and moving on Osaka castle in 1614 with a force of 164,000 men.
At that time Osaka castle was vast, with outer walls some 8 km in
circumference, 124 corner towers and moats 120 metres wide, more than
sufficient to accommodate the 114,000 Toyotomi supporters gathered inside.
Ieyasu had obtained a number of cannon, some from the Europeans whilst
others were Japanese-made, and he began bombarding the besieged castle.
After several weeks, during which little real damage was done to the

▲ Tokugawa Ieyasu commanding his troops during the Summer campaign against Osaka Castle.
By Kano Tanyu, about 1640. © Nikko Toshogu Shrine

massive walls, Ieyasu called for peace talks in which Toyotomi Hideyori agreed not to attempt any coup against the Tokugawa. With winter rapidly approaching Ieyasu returned to Edo, leaving behind a considerable number of troops to dismantle the outer walls of the castle and fill in the moats. Over the winter the Toyotomi supporters desperately tried to rebuild walls and dig out the moats but failed to complete the task. Using the rebuilding and the deliberate misreading of an inscription on a bell cast by the Toyotomi, Ieyasu had the excuses he needed to launch another attack the following summer. Although the Toyotomi had some initial successes as the Tokugawa force made its way towards Osaka, the final battle, fought outside the castle, resulted in Hideyori committing suicide as the castle burned.

With all potential threats eliminated, Tokugawa Ieyasu set about ensuring his family continued to maintain their hold on the shogunate. Branches of the family were established in the provinces of Kii, Mito and Owari provinces to supply heirs should the Edo branch fail to produce one. A vast network of spies reported happenings throughout the country and barriers were erected at strategic points on the road network preventing travel to those without the proper documentation. In 1616 Ieyasu died in his retirement home in Shizuoka, being buried there for a year until his mortuary shrine was ready at Nikko some 80 miles north of Edo.

▲ Nikko Toshogu Shrine. © Nikko Toshogu Shrine

◄ Imported Indian fabric used on an armour. Private collection

Ieyasu's son, Hidetada and his grandson Iemitsu were less tolerant of the Christians than Ieyasu had been, especially those of the Catholic faith. There was considerable concern over where the loyalty of Japanese Christians lay: was it to the *shogun* or to the pope? Persecutions of Catholic priests were followed by the confinement of all the foreign Catholics to a small artificial island called Dejima in Nagasaki harbour. Having been assured by the Dutch that they could maintain supplies of Chinese brocades, raw silk and other luxury goods, all foreigners except the Dutch were expelled from the country.

Further legislation banned the building of sea-going ships and all Japanese from leaving or re-entering the country on pain of death. Japanese Christians had to renounce their faith or suffer martyrdom. Japan had isolated itself from the world with the exception of the small Dutch colony on Dejima (a situation called *sakoku*).

One innovation initiated before Tokugawa Ieyasu's death was the insistence that all the *daimyo* should spend part of their time at the court in Edo. This practice became codified by the third Tokugawa *shogun* Iemitsu into one of the most characteristic institutions of Edo period Japan – that of 'alternate attendance' (*daimyo gyoretsu*). Depending on the distance of their lands from Edo, each *daimyo* had to spend half their time in service at the *shogun's* court. In addition, the wives and children of all *daimyo* had to live permanently in Edo, essentially as hostages. For the first time the title of *daimyo* was limited to those whose annual income was at least 10,000 koku of rice, the amount required to feed 10,000 people for a year. Those *daimyo* who had supported the Tokugawa at Seki ga Hara were classed as *fudai*

daimyo, or 'inside lords', with their mansions inside the outer walls of Edo castle. Those whose loyalty was suspect or who had opposed the Tokugawa were called *tozama daimyo* ('outside lords'), and had to build outside the castle precincts.

The stratification of the remainder of society, whilst already implicit, was now firmly codified in law. At the top of society were the *bushi* who formed a hierarchy headed by the *shogun*. Below these were the *daimyo*, followed by the various grades of *samurai*. Below these, in theory at least, came the farmers who grew food, followed by craftsmen who produced the goods upon which society depended. Finally, at the base of society, came the merchants who produced nothing. Unclassified were groups such as doctors, priests and others who performed duties regarded as defiling, such as leather working or dealing with the dead.

◄ Light folding armour often carried when travelling. Private collection and XXVIA.288

▲ A daimyo procession. From a 19th-century woodblock print. © Blackburn Museum

It was the *daimyo gyoretsu* that dominated the lives of many of the *bushi* during the Tokugawa period. Despite attempts by the authorities to limit the size of their retinues, the *daimyo* vied with each other to put on the most impressive display. The wealthier the *daimyo*, the greater the number of people involved and the more costly were their costumes and the accoutrements they carried. Although only a *tozama daimyo*, the Maeda family of Kaga province had an income of well over a million *koku* of rice, in part by trading with the Dutch. Up to 3,000 people were involved in the march to Edo. On a typical journey, the *daimyo* would be accompanied by more than a thousand *samurai*, of which 185 were immediate retainers and a further 830 more distant vassals. Attending the *samurai* were 686 servants and pages, and 286 grooms, handymen, cooks and administrative staff. They brought with them 32 horses from Kaga, hiring a further 188 from various post stations along the way. A poem of the period reads:

> The rear of the procession
> Vanished into the distant mist
> The Lord of Kaga.

The organisation of these processions was similar to that of an army marching to battle. Ahead of the procession proper was a party of clerks, handymen and cooks tasked with booking accommodation, preparing food and generally making all the arrangements for the evening. Official inns and post stations were spaced along the road system especially for this purpose. Heading the procession proper was an advanced guard led by two men carrying long spears with heraldic-shaped scabbards to indicate whose procession it was, together with others tasked with ensuring bystanders either retreated indoors or sank to their knees while the procession passed. Behind these came porters with large lacquered trunks on poles, and grooms leading pack horses that carried the luggage, each piece accompanied by attendants. Then came the retinues of the senior clan officials, men carrying spears, guns and bows. In the centre of the procession was the *daimyo* himself, carried in an enclosed palanquin and surrounded by his bodyguard carrying spears. Following him were his horses with their grooms and attendants. Finally came a large rearguard of armed retainers, servants often controlled by a senior councillor with his own retinue.

Each lord put on as brilliant a show as possible, providing colourful clothing and lavish equipment, much of which was specifically made for these events. Some staff weapons were made with shafts of lightweight wood, rather than the much heavier oak, the various metal fittings simulated with gilded paper to reduce the weight. All of the more costly items needed protection on these marches. Valuable swords were stored in bags of rich brocade and carried in lacquered wooden cases that in turn were protected by lacquered leather to protect the contents during inclement weather.

Most of the guns, by now symbols of prestige rather than for use, were carried in covers of lacquered leather or imported woollen cloth. The finest had lacquered cases similar to the swords. Some *daimyo* were reported to have ordered their gunners to carry a length of lighted match when passing through towns and cities to create a more martial effect, although few of those carrying the guns would have actually fired them. One simple device worn by most *samurai* was a pad called a *koshiate* that was worn under the sash to limit the pounding of the heavy swords on the hip bone when marching.

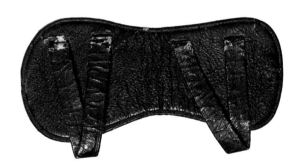

▲ A *koshiate*. Private collection

▶ Lacquered case and its leather cover for a long sword. Private collection

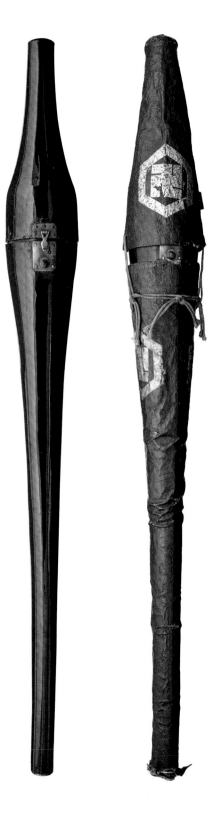

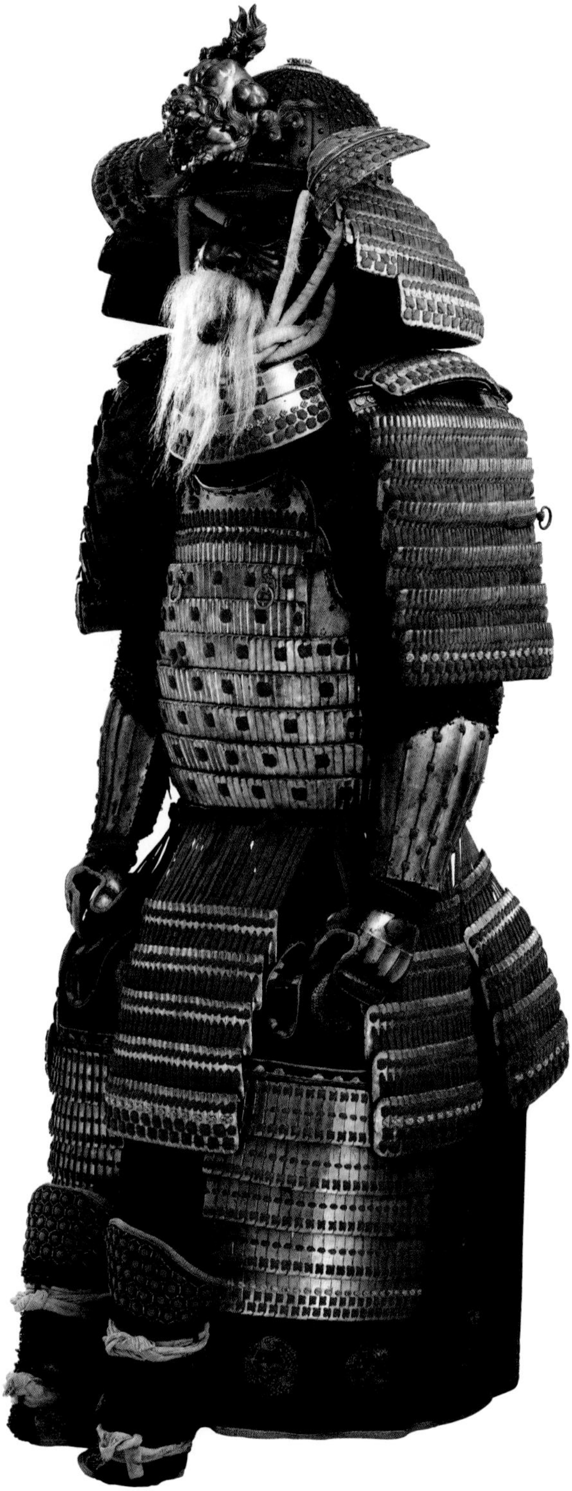

◀ Gold lacquered Edo-period armour.
XXVIA.247

As the decades of peace rolled by, decorative features began to reappear on armours. Stencilled leathers and soft metal mounts were re-introduced. Copies of the round helmet bowls worn with ancient armour were produced, often with prominent rivets and wide spreading neckguards that would have made the wearing of a *sashimono* impossible. By the second half of the 18th century there was a distinctly nostalgic movement for the glories of the past which led to copies of the old *do-maru*, *haramaki* and even *o-yoroi* being created for those who could afford the considerable expense. At first they were inaccurate pastiches, but by the end of the century near-perfect copies were being made.

► Helmet forged from a single plate. The coarse russet surface is overlaid with dragons, lightening and clouds in silver wire. XXVIA.98

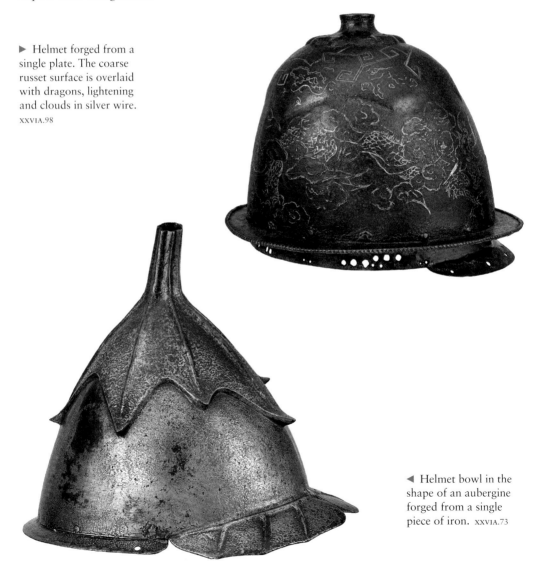

◄ Helmet bowl in the shape of an aubergine forged from a single piece of iron. XXVIA.73

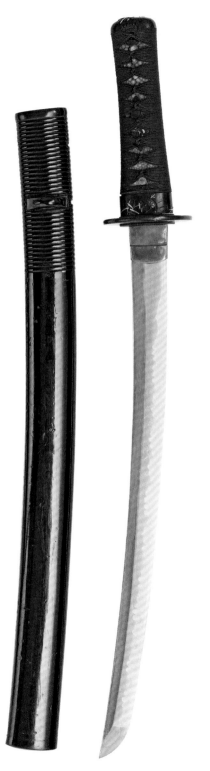

◀ Lacquered leather bad-weather cover for a sword hilt. Private collection

◀ *Left*: A *wakizashi* with scabbard. XXVIS.356

During this long period of enforced peace the arts of lacquer, metalwork, woodblock prints and textiles reached levels of artistic creativity that has only rarely been equalled elsewhere. Almost all *samurai* now wore their long swords, now called *katana*, thrust through their belt on the left hip, pairing it with either a dirk or a short sword called a *wakizashi*.

This was mounted like the *katana* and had a blade 30-61 cm long. Those with sufficient funds had the mounts of their *katana* and *wakizashi* made en suite, a combination called a *daisho*. Some of the more disreputable townsmen had swords made with blades below the official length for a *katana* worn in longer scabbards to give the impression they were *samurai* – a practice soon stamped on by the Tokugawa who issued a stream of edicts banning this and other excesses.

Sword fittings no longer had to withstand the knocks and damage of battle and, rather than iron, could be made from softer, more decorative metals and alloys. Craftsmen rose to the demand, creating tsuba and hilt fittings that are miniature works of art which have never been surpassed. Because the mounts of a sword could be changed, the rich sometimes had sets of mounts made for the same blade for use on different social occasions or seasons of the year. For centuries there had been a group of sword-fitting makers called the Goto who worked for the courts, creating designs executed in gold on a background of an alloy of gold and copper called *shakudo* chemically patinated to black. As the prosperity of the general population increased, *shakudo* and other alloys chosen for the colour they assumed when patinated began to be employed more widely.

These alloys gave the makers of fittings a considerable colour palette that included reds and browns from copper, greens and browns from bronzes and iron, greys from an alloy of silver and copper called *shibuichi*, black from *shakudo* as well as gold and silver themselves. Iron, always patinated with a controlled coating of rust, was chiselled in relief, apparently with the same facility as wood. Using inlaying and other techniques, masterpieces were created that might take for their themes scenes from history or legends, animals, birds, fish, plants or inanimate objects.

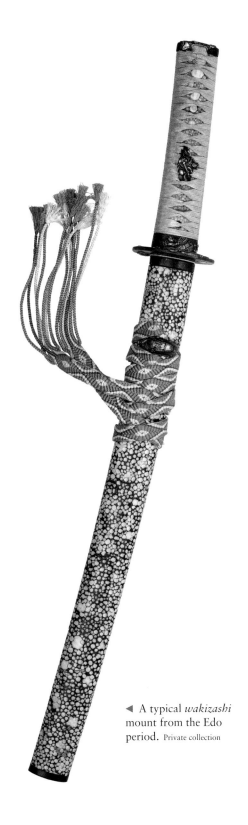

◀ A typical *wakizashi* mount from the Edo period. Private collection

Being a period of peace, the demand for swords during much of the Edo period (known as the *shinto* or 'new sword' era) was limited, and those blades that were made had rarely been used in action. To determine how they might perform in action, an official system of testing the efficacy of blades was instituted. The raw material for this grisly business called *tameshigiri* was generally a corpse from the execution grounds or, more rarely, a condemned criminal. With the corpse lying on a mound of sand and held in position by ties to bamboo poles, the tester would select one of the many cuts in his repertoire he thought the blade capable of. The simplest cuts would be through a wrist or limb, the most difficult through the pelvic region of diagonally from shoulder to hip. On completing the cut, the blade and corpse would be examined and the details of a successful test chiselled on the tang of the blade.

By the late 18th century a group of swordsmiths, echoing the production of ancient styles of armours, initiated a return to what they regarded as a golden age of sword production of the *koto* period by imitating the blades of the past. Known as the *shinshinto* or 'new-new sword era', one of its leading lights was a smith called Suishinshi Masahide who soon gathered around him a group of like-minded smiths. Although many superb blades were produced, none really managed to emulate the blades of the past.

▼ An iron sword guard or *tsuba* representing a goose and clouds against the moon. XXVIS.373

▲ An iron sword guard or *tsuba* chiselled with cherry blossom. XXVIS.385

THE FINAL FLOWERING
(1853 AND BEYOND)

In 1844 the Dutch King sent a letter to the *shogun* via the trading post on Dejima suggesting that Japan should consider opening ports to foreign ships. This followed several attempts to make landings during which ships had been driven away. Matters came to a head in 1852 when the Americans sent a fleet of four ships under the command of Commodore Matthew Perry to deliver a letter to the *shogun* demanding a trading treaty. The answer was to be ready the following year, and during the ensuing panic, preparations were made to repulse the foreigners and coastal defences were strengthened with mortars and other guns purchased from the Dutch. Many *samurai* had sensible armours made in the style of the Sengoku era, expecting to have to fight what was viewed as an invasion. The following year Perry returned for his answer, this time landing on Japanese soil and parading marines armed with modern guns. The large force of *samurai* that had assembled could only stand by impotently.

Over the next decade or so there was turmoil as Japan tried to come to terms with the modern world. Discontent with the inequality of the treaties extracted from the Tokugawa resulted in the emperor taking part in matters of state for the first time in centuries, encouraged by the clans of Nagato, Tosa and Satsuma. The *shogun*, Tokugawa Yoshinobu, initially abdicated in favour of the emperor, but disturbances in Edo and an imperial decree abolishing the house of Tokugawa caused him to send a force to take Kyoto. There followed a series of campaigns in which the Westerners assisted the imperial forces, leading to the defeat of the Tokugawa and ultimately a country unified under the Emperor Meiji.

◀ *Opposite*: A *samurai* with his bow. I.303

▲ Pistol ignited by detonating pellets.
XXVIF.230

The initial reaction of the Japanese to the opening of the country was to reject much of their traditional culture. Missions were sent around the world to study modern politics, technology, science and culture. Many adopted Western dress wearing their swords rather incongruously with frock coats and top hats. In 1876 the emperor issued the Haitorei Edict, formally abolishing the feudal system and banning the wearing of swords except by the police and military. The last *shoguns* had admired the armies of the French, importing equipment to establish a bodyguard dressed in the breastplates and plumed helmets of cuirassiers. The defeat of the French in the Franco-Prussian war resulted in Meiji modelling his new army on that of Germany and his navy on that of Britain. For a time the army issued mass-produced swords based on cavalry swords used in Europe, but these were quickly replaced by a style of mounting called *kyu gunto* having a long hilt with a knucklebow that would accommodate an old blade. Swords of this type were used during both the Sino-Japanese and Russo-Japanese wars.

In 1934, the rise in militarism saw a new sword mount, the type 94 or *shin gunto*, devised for army officers. It was based on the style of *tachi* used during the Kamakura era. This new pattern of sword had a rayskin and silk-wrapped wooden hilt with brass mounts decorated with cherry blossoms. It also had a brass *tsuba* and a wood-lined metal scabbard with two suspension rings, one of which was removable for ordinary wear. Because of its construction and style, it was possible to carry a traditional blade in these mounts, although many contained modern factory-made blades. The navy too wore similar swords called *kaigunto* but with a different pattern of mounts and scabbards that were covered with lacquered fish-skin. Because of the conditions at sea, these swords often had blades of stainless steel.

In 1935 a similar sword to the type 94, the *kyugo shiki gunto*, was issued to non-commissioned officers. These had mass-produced factory-made blades and hilts of cast copper or aluminium painted to look like a traditional bound hilt. Finally, in 1938, a simplified version of the *shin gunto*, the type 98, was authorised; it differed mainly in only having one suspension ring. When war broke out in 1939 it is estimated that there were two million troops who were required to wear swords as part of their uniform. To meet this need, traditional smiths who had managed to keep their craft alive since the days of the Emperor Meiji turned out hundreds of thousands of blades as their contribution to the war effort. To avoid the labour involved in forging traditional *tamahagane*, most of the blades were forged from old steel (often sections of railway line). Smiths found that by repeatedly heating and quenching this steel a grain similar to that visible on traditional blades could be created. The resulting billet could then be shaped and quenched in the established way to produce a blade that was very similar to a traditionally-produced one.

Following Japan's defeat in 1945, America expressed its intention to destroy all Japanese swords as reparation for the war. Hundreds of thousands of swords were rounded up from temples, shrines and families, and stockpiled in centres to await destruction. Fortunately, common sense prevailed. Traditional swords were reprieved, although only after a considerable number had been sent to the furnaces. By the 1950s, as memories of the war receded the attitude towards swords softened, and smiths once again began to produce blades. Today the craft of swordmaking has been re-established and swords are once again being made in ways that stand comparison with those of the past.

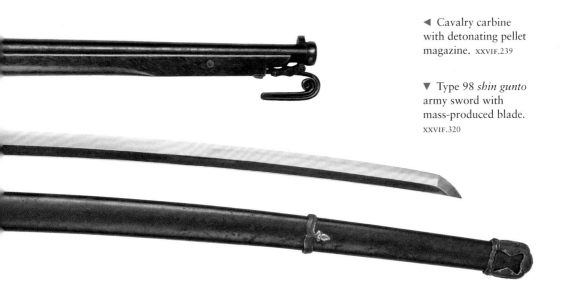

◀ Cavalry carbine with detonating pellet magazine. XXVIF.239

▼ Type 98 *shin gunto* army sword with mass-produced blade. XXVIF.320

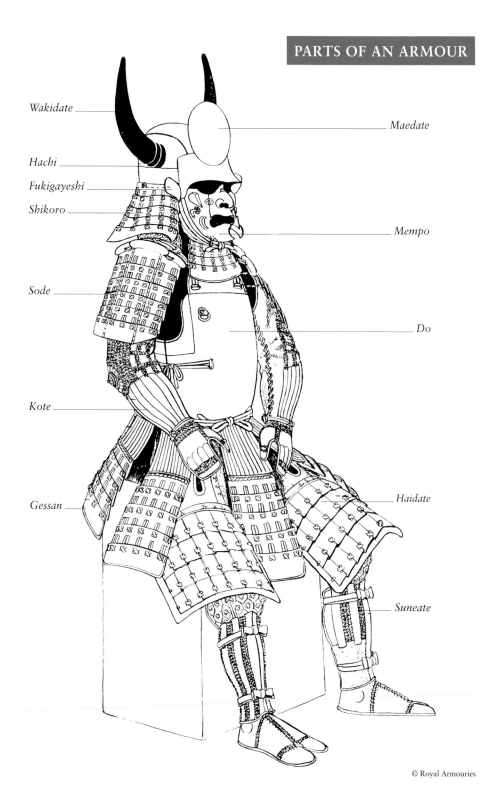

Wakidate

Hachi

Fukigayeshi

Shikoro

Sode

Kote

Gessan

Maedate

Mempo

Do

Haidate

Suneate

© Royal Armouries

GLOSSARY

abumi	the type of stirrup used by the Japanese
agemaki	an ornate tasselled bow attached to the back of an armour
akodanari kabuto	a form of helmet having a bulbous swelling to rear part of the bowl
aori gawa	a pair of roughly rectangular leather panels hanging from the saddle rings
ashigaru	'light foot', a common solider armed with a gun
bajo zutsu	carbines
buke	the warrior class
bushi	a warrior
daimyo	territorial lords
daimyo gyoretsu	feudal lord's procession to and from Edo during the Tokugawa period
daisho	a matched pair of long and short swords
do	armour that covered the body
do maru	a lamellar armour that closes under the right arm
ebira	an open-framed quiver
fukigayeshi	the turnbacks at the front edge of a neck guard
gendaito	'military-era swords', about 1876 – 1953
gessan	the defence for the hips and thighs of a modern armour, see also *kusazuri*
go mai do	a cuirass that divides into five pieces
gokaden	the five major traditions of sword making before 1600
gusoku	later term for an armour
gyoyo	a leaf-shaped plate originally devised to protect the shoulders but later the fastenings of the shoulder straps
habaki	a collar around the base of a blade that transmits the shock of a blow to the hilt
hachi	the bowl of a helmet

hada	the grain visible in the steel of a blade
hadome	cross guard fitted to a spear shaft or a flange on the cheeks of a face mask
haidate	defence for the thighs, generally in the form of a divided apron
hamon	the shape of the hardened edge of a blade
haramaki	an armour that fastens at the back
harikaki kabuto	helmet built up with lacquered paper etc to resemble some fanciful object
hata	a flag
hinawaju	one of several names for a matchlock gun
hineno zunari kabuto	a head-shaped helmet with the top plate running under the brow-plate
hira ne	flat, shield-shaped arrow head
hirumaki	the shaft of a staff weapon wrapped with a spiral of leather
hoko	a spear blade with a single side blade
hoshi	a rivet
ita	a plate
iyo zane	wide scales assembled with almost no overlap
jinbaori	a fabric surcoat worn over armour
jumonji yari	spear with side blades, see also *mogari yari*
kabuto	a helmet
kago yumi	small bow carried in a palanquin see also *riman kyu*
kaji	a sword smith
kakae zutsu	a variety of large bore guns, see also *o-zutsu*
kamon	an heraldic device
kanamono	a generic term for any ornamental metalwork
karimata	a forked arrowhead
kashi	Japanese red oak
katana	a long sword with a blade longer than 61 cm, worn edge upwards in the sash on the left hip

katana kake	a sword rack	naginata	a staff weapon with a single edged curved blade similar to a glaive
katchu	a generic term for armour see also *yoroi* and *gusoku*	nakagawa	those rows of scales or plates of a cuirass that encircle the torso
katchu shi	an armourer	nakago	the tang of a sword or spear blade
kebiki odoshi	the style of lacing used for scale armour	nanako	a surface texture on ornamental metalwork produced by a small cup punch
kikuchi yari	an early form of single edged spear		
kiritsuke kozane	the modelling of armour plates with lacquer to look like a row of scales	ni mai do	a cuirass that divides into two sections, front and back, joined by a hinge
koshi ate	a pad to protect the hip when wearing a sword	nobori	a very tall narrow flag indicating a headquarters on a battlefield
koshimaki	an iron strip riveted to lower edge of a helmet bowl	o-yoroi	a lamellar armour provided with a separate plate to cover the right side
kote	armoured sleeve		
koto	sword made before 1600	odoshi ge	the material used for lacing an armour
kura	saddle		
kusari	mail	okkashi gusoku	a 'lent armour', issued by a lord
kusazuri	the defence for the hips and upper thighs of a lamellar armour, see also *gessan*	sabi nuri	lacquer finish imitating russet iron
		samé	skin of a ray
kutsu wa	Japanese bit	samurai	military retainer of feudal nobleman
kuwagata	horn-like crests attached to the front of a helmet	sane	a lamellae or scale from which armour was assembled
kyu	a bow		
kyudo	the practice of archery	sankaku yari	a spearhead of triangular section
mabezashi	the peak of a helmet	sashimono	an identification flag or other device fastened to the back plate of an armour
mae date	a crest attached to the front of a helmet		
mekugi	the peg of horn or bamboo that holds a blade into the hilt	saya	a scabbard
		sei ita	a narrow plate to protect back opening of *haramaki*
mempo	a mask covering the face and nose below the eyes		
		sengoku jidai	the 'Age of the Country at War', about 1470 – 1630
men gu	face armour		
menuki	metal ornaments under the binding of a sword hilt to assist the grip	seppa	ornate, soft metal washers fitted on either side of a sword guard
		shaku	a unit of measurement equivalent to 11.93 inches
mogami gusoku	armour on which each plate in the *nakagawa* is individually hinged	shakudo	an alloy of copper and gold that patinates to a black colour
momme	a unit of weight (1000 momme = 3.75 kg)	shikoro	the neck guard of the helmet
mon	heraldic device, see also *kamon*	shinshin to	a sword made towards the end of the feudal period
mune ita	the upper plate at the front of a cuirass	shin to	a sword made after 1600 but before the *shinshin to* era
nagamaki	a long, straight bladed staff weapon	shira no ya	a whistling arrow

shogun	the military ruler of Japan
sode	a shoulder guard
su yari	simple spears
sugake odoshi	armour lacing using spaced pairs of laces
suji	a standing flange on the edge of a plate making up a helmet
suneate	shin guards
tachi	a long sword worn with the cutting edge downward
tamahagane	spongy mixture of iron, steel and slag from the smelting furnace
tameshi giri	the testing of a sword
tanegashima	a name for a gun named after the place where they were first made
tanto	a dirk or dagger with a blade less than 1 *shaku* in length (less than 30 cm)
tehen	the hole in the top of a helmet
tehen kanamono	the ornament surrounding the hole in the top of a helmet
teppo	one of many terms for a gun
tosei gusoku	armour styles that came into use in the Sengoku period

tsuba	a sword guard
tsubo sode	shoulder guards that narrow towards the bottom
tsuka	the hilt of a sword
uchigatana	a 'striking sword', an ancestor of the *katana*
urushi	lacquer
utsubo	fully-enclosed quiver used in bad weather
waidate	a solid plate covering the right side of the body of an *o-yoroi*
wakizashi	a sword having a blade length between 1 and 2 *shaku* (about 30-61 cm)
ya	arrow
ya no ne	arrowheads
yakiba	the hardened cutting edge of a blade
yari	spear
yoroi	armour, especially lamellar armour
yoroi hitatare	costume worn under an armour
yumi	bow
zunari kabuto	head-shaped helmet

FURTHER READING

Japanese armour

Anderson, L J 1968 *Japanese armour: An illustrated guide to the work of the Myochin and Saotome families from the fifteenth to the twentieth century.* London, Arms and Armour Press

Bottomley, I 1998 *Japanese Armor: the Galeno collection.* Berkeley, Stonebridge Press

Bottomley, I and **Hopson, A P** 1988 *Arms and armour of the samurai.* London, Defoe Publishing

Kaneda Chapplear, K 1987 *Japanese armour makers for the samurai.* Tokyo, Miyoshi Printing Co.

Robinson, H R 1962 *The manufacture of armour and helmets in sixteenth-century Japan* [a translation of *Chukokatchu Seisakuben* by Sakakibara Kozan]. London, Holland Press

Robinson, H R 1964 *The armour book in Honcho Gunkiko.* London, Holland Press

Robinson, H R 1967 *Oriental armour*. London, Herbert Jenkins Ltd

Robinson, H R 1969 *Japanese arms and armour*. London, Arms and Armour Press

Japanese swords

Bottomley I 2002 *Introduction to Japanese armour*. Leeds, Royal Armouries

Fuller F and Gregory R 1986 *Military swords of Japan 1868-1945*. London, Arms and Armour Press

Inami M 1948 *Nippon To: the Japanese sword*. Tokyo, Japan Sword Co. Ltd

Irvine, G 2000 *The Japanese sword; soul of the samurai*. London, V&A Publications

Sinclair, C 2001 *Samurai, the weapons and spirit of the Japanese warrior*. London, Salamander Books Ltd

Yamagami, H 1941 *Japan's ancient armour*. Tokyo, Japanese Government Railways

Kapp, L H and Yoshihara, Y 1987 *The craft of the Japanese sword*. Tokyo, Kodansha International

Robinson, B W 1961 *The arts of the Japanese sword*. London, Faber & Faber

Sato, K 1983 *The Japanese sword*. Tokyo, Kodansha International

Yumoto, J 1958 *The Samurai sword*. Rutland VT, Tuttle

Published by Royal Armouries Museum, Armouries Drive, Leeds LS10 1LT, United Kingdom

www.royalarmouries.org

Ian Bottomley has asserted his right under the Copyright, Designs and Patent Act (1988) to be identified as the author of this book.

ISBN 978 0 948092 79 4

Edited by Martyn Lawrence

Designed by Geraldine Mead

Photography by Gary Ombler, Rod Joyce

Printed by W &G Baird Ltd

10 9 8 7 6 5 4 3

A CIP record for this book is available from the British Library

Every effort has been made to trace the copyright holders of images, where applicable. Any errors or omissions are unintentional, and the publisher will be pleased to insert any appropriate acknowledgements in future editions.

FSC
www.fsc.org
MIX
Paper from responsible sources
FSC® C016201